RAFAEL ALBERTI
SELECTED POEMS

RAFAEL ALBERTI
SELECTED POEMS

Edited and Translated by
BEN BELITT

Introduction by
LUIS MONGUIÓ

UNIVERSITY OF CALIFORNIA PRESS
Berkeley and Los Angeles   1966

© 1966 by The Regents of the University of California

University of California Press
Berkeley and Los Angeles, California

Cambridge University Press
London, England

Rafael Alberti's poems have been published
and copyrighted in Spanish by Editorial Losada, S.A.,
Buenos Aires, 1941, 1944, 1948, 1952, 1953, and 1954
His drawings are
reproduced from *Entre el clavel y
la espada*, copyright 1941 by Editorial
Losada, S.A.

La arboleda perdida (A *Vanished Grove*) was
published in Buenos Aires in 1959 by General
Fabril Editora

Library of Congress Catalog Card Number: 65–25327

FOR LUIS MONGUIÓ

Erudito vivo, amigo de la poesía, amigo

CONTENTS

The Poetry of Rafael Alberti: An Introduction
By Luis Monguió 1

Translator's Preface, by Ben Belitt 35

A Vanished Grove: 1 47

CAL Y CANTO / QUICKLIME AND SONG (1929) ... 51

   Carta abierta / Open Letter 52
   Guía estival del paraíso / Summer Guidebook
     to Paradise 58
   Madrigal al billete del tranvía / Madrigal on a
     Tram Ticket 60

A Vanished Grove: 2 64

SOBRE LOS ÁNGELES / CONCERNING
ANGELS (1929) 67

   Paraíso perdido / Paradise Lost 68
   El ángel falso / False Angel 70
   El ángel bueno / The Good Angel 74
   Los ángeles colegiales / Grammar School Angels ... 74
   El ángel de los números / The Angel of Number ... 76
   Los ángeles mohosos / Angels of Mildew ... 78
   Los ángeles muertos / The Dead Angels ... 78
   El ángel mentiroso / Deceiving Angel 80
   El ángel avaro / Angel of Avarice 82
   Canción del ángel sin suerte / Song of the Un-
     lucky Angel 84
   El ángel de carbón / Angel of Coals 84
   El ángel rabioso / Angel Enraged 86

CONTENTS

  El ángel desengañado / Angel Undeceived   88
  El ángel ángel / Angel's Angel   88
  El alma en pena / Soul in Torment   90

SERMONES Y MORADAS / SERMONS AND
SOJOURNS (1930)   95

  Sermón de la sangre / Sermon on Blood   96

A Vanished Grove: 3   98

VERTE Y NO VERTE / TO HAVE SEEN YOU
AND SEE YOU NO MORE (1935)   103

  Elegía / Elegy   104
  El toro de la muerte (1) / The Bull of Death (1)
  El toro de la muerte (2) / The Bull of Death (2)
  El toro de la muerte (3) / The Bull of Death (3)
  El toro de la muerte (4) / The Bull of Death (4)
  Dos arenas / Two Sands

A Vanished Grove: 4   124

CAPITAL DE LA GLORIA / CAPITAL OF GLORY
(1938)   127

  Los soldados se duermen / Soldiers Asleep   128
  Los campesinos / Country Recruits   128
  Monte de El Pardo / On the Slopes of El Pardo   130
  A "Niebla", mi perro / To Misty, My Dog   132

ENTRE EL CLAVEL Y LA ESPADA / BETWEEN
SWORD AND CARNATION (1941)   137

  De ayer para hoy / From Yesterday for Today   138
  Sonetos corporales: 3 / Corporeal Sonnets: 3   138
  Sonetos corporales: 7 / Corporeal Sonnets: 7   140

CONTENTS

    De los álamos y los sauces / From Poplar and Willow   142
        10: *Anda serio ese hombre* / A man with a taciturn air   142
        14: *Perdidos, ay, perdidos!* / Fallen! O fallen!   144
    Del pensamiento en mi jardín / From Thoughts in A Garden   146

PLEAMAR / FLOODTIDE (1944)   149

    Tirteo / Tyrtaeus   150
    Cuando se nos va alguien / When Someone Is Lost to Us   154

A Vanished Grove: 5   160

A LA PINTURA / HOMAGE TO PAINTING (1948)   163
    A la paleta / A Palette   164
    Negro / Black   164
    Azul / Blue   168
    Rojo / Red   172
    Blanco / White   174
    Al pincel / A Paintbrush   178
    Velázquez / Velázquez   180
    Miguel Ángel / Michelangelo   186

A Vanished Grove: 6   194

RETORNOS DE LO VIVO LEJANO / RETURNS OF THE FAR AND THE LIVING (1952)   195

    Retornos del ángel de sombra / Returns: Dark Angel   196
    Retornos del amor en los vividos paisajes / Love's Returns: An Inhabited Landscape   196
    Retornos de una sombra maldita / Returns: A Shadow Accursed   200

CONTENTS

Retornos de un poeta asesinado / Returns: A Poet Murdered ... 202
Retornos del amor en el palco de teatro / Love's Returns: A Theater Loge ... 204

COPLAS DE JUAN PANADERO / BROADSIDES FOR JUAN PANADERO (1949–1953) ... 209

Poética de Juan Panadero / Juan Panadero: Poetics ... 210

Baladas y Canciones del Paraná / Ballads and Songs of the Paraná (1953–1954) ... 215

Canción 8 / Song 8 ... 216
Balada del andaluz perdido / Ballad of the Lost Andalusian ... 216

THE POETRY OF RAFAEL ALBERTI: AN INTRODUCTION

Translated by Ben Belitt

Rafael Alberti is by no means unknown to English-speaking readers throughout the world. It was in 1944 however, that Lloyd Malan first published his brief pamphlet of selections from Alberti in the New Directions Poet of the Month Series, and scarcely a year later that Eleanor L. Turnbull's anthology appeared in which Alberti was one of ten Spanish poets published in English. Other versions, in verse and in prose, have followed at irregular intervals.[1] Today, Rafael Alberti in 1965 is still considerably less well-known—and translated—than his talents, which are distinctive and indisputable, deserve. The present volume of Ben Belitt's is, to the best of my knowledge, the only collection which makes available to English readers the striking range and variety of this poet, in firm English verse and in the language of their

[1] *Selected Poems of Rafael Alberti*, trans. by Lloyd Malan (New York: New Directions, 1944), 32 pp.; *Contemporary Spanish Poetry, Selections from Ten Poets*, trans. by Eleanor L. Turnbull, with Spanish Originals, and Personal Reminiscences of the Poets by Pedro Salinas (Baltimore: Johns Hopkins Press, 1945), pp. 237–277; *The Penguin Book of Spanish Verse*, ed. and trans. by J. M. Cohen (Harmondsworth, Eng., 1952), pp. 400–408; *Thirty Spanish Poems of Love and Exile*, trans. by Kenneth Rexroth (San Francisco: City Lights Books, 1957), pp. 1–10.

INTRODUCTION

originals. My part in this venture is to orient the accomplishment of Alberti, in both its exceptional and traditional aspects, to the history of Castilian poetry as a whole, like a point on the imaginative map of his country.

1

Unquestionably, the constellation of poets that appeared between 1920 and 1936 is the most extraordinary in the annals of Spanish letters since the epoch of Garcilaso, Herrera, Fray Luis de León, and St. John of the Cross in the sixteenth century, and the era of Lope and Góngora and Quevedo and Calderón in the seventeenth. In that galaxy of talents, often called the "Generation of 1927," poets born in the last years of the nineteenth century and the first years of our own, predominate: Gerardo Diego (1896), Federico García Lorca (1898), Vicente Aleixandre (1898), Emilio Prados (1899), Rafael Alberti (1902), Luis Cernuda (1904). Closely related, if somewhat older, are three earlier poets: José Moreno Villa (1887), Pedro Salinas (1892), and Jorge Guillén (1893); and presiding over the whole pantheon, as *dii penates* of the modern, are three older masters: Miguel de Unamuno (1864), Antonio Machado (1875), and Juan Ramón Jiménez (1881). Add to these the younger but equally gifted poet of the '30's, Miguel Hernández (1910), and you have a roll call at once brilliant, barely credible, and—in the hindsight that reveals how prodigiously Spain nurtures and expends its great talents—sad: Lorca tragically dead in 1936, and Hernández in 1942; Unamuno dead, in spiritual

INTRODUCTION

isolation, in 1936. Machado dead in exile in 1939, Salinas in 1951, Moreno Villa in 1954, Juan Ramón Jiménez in 1958, Prados in 1962, and Cernuda in 1963: all dead. Time has preserved for us, still alive in their native Spain, Diego and Aleixandre, and those Spanish pilgrims to the New World, Guillén and Alberti—all stars of the first magnitude whose luster need never grow dim.

It must not be assumed from this that fine poets ceased to exist in Spain between its golden centuries and the twentieth century. The eighteenth century had its Jovellanos and Meléndez Valdés; the nineteenth, its Quintana, Espronceda, Bécquer. There existed also significant groups like the neoclassicist coteries of Seville and Salamanca, and the romantic Pleiades; but the point to be emphasized here is that rarely, in Spain or outside it, have so many gifted poets appeared in a comparable space of time, each one distinct in endowment and sensibility, yet all in rapport. The phenomenon is all the more striking if one reflects that in 1870, with the death of Gustavo Adolfo Bécquer (the "Heine of Spain," some have called him) it began to appear that lyricism in the Castilian language had exhausted its resources—that only in Galician, in Rosalía de Castro, or in Catalan, in Verdaguer and Maragall, had a poetry worthy of the name survived on the Iberian mainland.

Certainly in the last quarter of the nineteenth century, good verse was being written in Castilian; the substance, however, was prosaic: oratorical pieces in the style of parliamentary discourse, or little rhymed homilies propounding the bourgeois philosophy.

INTRODUCTION

Doubtless, they reflected the tastes of a Bourbon Restoration society (vintage 1875), for better or worse—the timid jargon of liberalism that camouflaged a no less pusillanimous conservatism. Justification of a sort may be found in the fact that Spain, after decades of wearisome vicissitude, needed to lie fallow; but the negative consequences are far more apparent, in a waning of faith in the destiny of Spain and its people. It was the era when it was possible to speak of Spain's "failure of nerve"; when a philosophy of the future could be erected on the premise that "nothing in Spain could not worsen, though the worst was already at hand." It was a period wholly unpropitious for poetic exaltation. In those days novelists were writing in Spain in a prose worthy of the literary tradition of Spanish realism, and, in the case of Benito Pérez Galdós, worthy of the best prose literature of Europe in his century. Poetry, however, was another matter, and, as has been pointed out, was lost to the language after Bécquer—that elegist, at once so touching, intimate, and simple, of the imperfection and mutability of love, life, and all things terrestrial; of the inaccessibility of perfection and of poetry itself.

It is in contrast to this hiatus of 1870–1900 that the first decades of the twentieth century launched a startling reaffirmation of poetry in Spanish. How, and for what reasons?

2

The year 1898 is a bounding line, dividing and clarifying all. The disaster of the Spanish-American War shocked the nation out of its apathy. The

INTRODUCTION

blowing up of the *Maine* in the port of Havana was a blessing in disguise in the spiritual history of Spain. Spain's defeat at the hands of the United States was one of those catastrophes that shake a nation to its roots and either force fresh sap into dry sticks, or leave it to wither away among the community of living nations. In the case of Spain, the disaster of '98 accomplished the former.

It is a curious truth that Spain owes its rebirth to that very "Generation of '98" which later generations came to regard—because of a seeming absence of action and will—as remiss in its destiny. It was this generation of the youth of '98—angry, ashamed, and frustrated—that examined and debated the "problem of Spain" with passionate intensity, if not, indeed, with that "strong feeling," that "overflow of powerful emotions" and exaltation that Wordsworth called the basis of all poetry. For this very reason, perhaps, the literature of Spain between 1898 and 1936 is predominantly poetic. Precisely as verse dwindled away into prose in the last quarter of the nineteenth century, the first third of our own century turned even its prose into poetry. The work of Valle-Inclán, Azorín, Miró, and Pérez de Ayala bears witness to this truth; and if Ortega y Gasset is a fitting example, even the philosophers of Spain were poets-in-prose. Small reason to wonder, in an atmosphere such as this, that poets reappeared on the scene and devoted their whole force to the writing not of verse, but of poems!

In the years of agonized self-scrutiny, Spain, shorn of false pride, accepted for the first time the literary influences that came to it from the lands beyond the

INTRODUCTION

seas where poets of the countries born of her former colonies were revolutionizing poetic expression in the grain of the language itself. In 1898, the very year of the Spanish debacle, the Nicaraguan poet, Rubén Darío, went to Spain and preached his new evangel of "modernism" to the young. Two of the masters who appeared on the Peninsula in the first decade of the twentieth century, Antonio Machado and Juan Ramón Jiménez, were greatly in his debt. Darío himself, in the course of his visits to Spain, was "Hispanicized" in his turn, thus deepening his influence on a generation of Spaniards obsessed with the destiny of their nation. Let me go a step further and say that the progressive Hispanization of Darío—evident in his *Cantos de vida y esperanza* (1905)—led to the irony of Machado's early disengagement from the example of Darío, the Darío of *Prosas profanas* (1896) and its cosmopolitan accessories. Juan Ramón Jiménez, a poet of more elegant sensibility than Machado and therefore closer to the art of Darío, carried the mark of the American on his poetic idiom well into the second decade of this century. It was then that he stripped his poetry of external influence, though never abandoning his quest for the expression of "pure inner rhythm," a quest so well learned of his master that he soon passed beyond it and found his own means of attaining it.

Thus, the poets in Spain who began publishing in the third decade of this century—Salinas, Guillén, Lorca, and the others cited, including Alberti—are all direct heirs of Darío, Machado, and Jiménez; and what they inherited was the predisposition to poetry made possible by the Generation of '98. Needless to say,

INTRODUCTION

other elements contributed to the fabric of their art; but the musicality, the sensuous texture, and the conscious technique of Darío, the progressive purification of poetic perception of Juan Ramón Jiménez, the passion for life and for truth, the profound love of Spain, the scrupulous integrity of feeling and intelligence of Antonio Machado (and his friend, Unamuno)—all were models so thoroughly mastered and assimilated by the young, that, adding their personal gift to what was already given, they could leave all behind them and forge ahead on their own.

While augmenting the wealth of immediate tradition, the Generation of '27 uncovered new sources of power and built them directly into the matrix of their poetics. They delved into the Hispanic past, acknowledging all that was most authentic and congenial in the popular inflection still preserved in their oral tradition, as well as in the poetry collections of the fifteenth and sixteenth centuries; or in those of the art ballads of the seventeenth, all newly brought into prominence by scholarly revaluation. To this was joined a fascination with the techniques of Baroque lyricism, celebrated and extended on the occasion of the tercentenaries of Góngora (1927) and Lope de Vega (1935), and with the more intimate romanticism of Bécquer, whose centennial they prepared for in 1936.

At the same time, Spain increasingly opened a perspective on the world beyond the Pyrenees, as youthful poets left for other parts of Europe and for the Americas, some of them on government scholarships, others as teachers of Spanish in foreign universities, and still others as literary tourists. Paris, London, Berlin, New York, Buenos Aires were no longer remote names on a map, dreamingly idealized; the literature of those foreign parts was no longer a matter of a few and far-between books; foreign poets were no longer mythical and marvelous, yet personally unknown, beings. Suddenly all became facts of their common experience, of their day-to-day reading, of frequent immediate conversation—friends with whom ideas and experiments were debated as among equals, free to agree or disagree as they pleased. Futurism, Dadaism, Ultraism, Creationism, Surrealism, Purism, Vitalism were formulas both national and cosmopolitan, examined between jest and earnest now in Parisian Left Bank cafés, now in the cafés on the Calle de Alcalá in Madrid, sometimes in an Oxford or Cambridge college, sometimes in Madrid's Residencia de Estudiantes.

The pages of the *Revista de Occidente,* of *La Gaceta Literaria,* of *Cruz y Raya,* the literary book section of a daily newspaper like *El Sol* show the poets of '27 come of age, secure in the worldwide validity of the voice and tradition of Spain on the one hand, and certain of the value of their own and unique contemporary experience on the other, testing their minds and poetic sensibilities in a world where "modern poetry" was an international phenomenon.

At that moment of the literary fulfillment of a generation, the Civil War of 1936–1939 exploded in Spain. Its result was a devastating dispersal of talent; and it was at this time (1940) that Alberti sought refuge in Argentina.

3

Rafael Alberti was born on December 16, 1902, in Puerto de Santa María near the shores of that Bay of Cádiz which Juan Ramón Jiménez was to call, in the same words with which he characterized the early poems of Alberti, an "uninterrupted upsurge of the beautiful, with odors, essences, sea-spray and music in miraculous variety."[2] His grandparents were Italians who had settled in Spain in the nineteenth century, and exported Andalusian wines throughout Europe as far north as Sweden and Russia. At the time of Alberti's birth, his branch of the family had come upon hard times, and his father was employed as a traveling salesman for a Jerez winery; nevertheless, the family still preserved a genteel decorum. Rafael attended private primary schools in El Puerto, and spent four out of a regimen of six secondary school years in a fashionable Jesuit institution in his native city. Unable to afford the expense of boarding school status, he was enrolled by the Jesuit fathers as a charity day student, and thereby felt himself looked down upon by both his teachers and his resident classmates, children of well-to-do parents. One can readily imagine the psychological scars left on the child by this experience, the resentments both conscious and subconscious it unleashed; and eventually, the effect of his status as a *déclassé* adolescent on his later preoccupation with movements advocating the classless society.

In 1917, his family was compelled to move to

[2] Letter of Juan Ramón Jiménez to Rafael Alberti, May 31, 1925, in *Marinero en tierra* (Madrid, 1925), p. 124.

INTRODUCTION

Madrid, a change which to Rafael seemed a calamitous deprival. In the capital, however, he was to discover the delights of the Prado, and dedicate himself with a passion to painting. Not until 1921 did he begin to write his first poems, which found their way into "little magazines" in 1922 and 1923. The manuscript of his first volume, *Marinero en tierra*, published in 1925, won him the national prize for poetry for 1924–1925. The jury who singled it out for that honor included a master-scholar, Ramón Menéndez Pidal, the poets Antonio Machado and José Moreno Villa, an author of excellent comedies, Carlos Arniches, and a novelist of distinction, Gabriel Miró. No poet of his years could want for a more distinguished panel of godfathers to preside over his public debut.

Suddenly, at twenty-two, thanks to his national prize, the coteries of Madrid looked toward Alberti as a young poet of great expectations and admitted him readily to the literary elite, the café talk of artists and writers, the theatrical greenrooms, the editorial rooms of periodicals and newspapers of a great capital. Together with poets like Lorca and Guillén, painters like Salvador Dalí, moviemakers like Luis Buñuel—friends of his, all of them—his situation was stellar.

In 1926, 1927, and 1929, new collections flowed from his pen to the presses. One of them, *Cal y canto*, with the canonical imprint of the *Revista de Occidente* and the blessings of its editor Ortega y Gasset, carried with it the maximum prestige possible in Madrid in 1929. In that same year there appeared another title, one of the most important he was to produce: *Sobre los ángeles*. Meanwhile, in the midst of

INTRODUCTION

a deepening personal crisis to which this book bears witness, he was fortunate enough to fall in love with Maríá Teresa León, a writer in her own right and since then his constant companion.

Up until this time, Alberti had lived, as he says, "wholly removed from political uproar"; but by the end of the third decade of this century, only the grossly insensitive could continue to exist apart from the political tensions of Spain: professors and students, sergeants and generals, intellectuals and workers—all were keyed to the growing momentousness of the hour. According to Alberti, it was the student revolts against the regime of General Miguel Primo de Rivera that first opened his eyes to the national peril and mustered his political awareness, then somewhat confused and anarchical.[3]

The "problem of Spain," launched decades before by the Generation of '98, began to bear new fruit, in a guise that even the most engaged of that generation would not have anticipated, horrifying some of its survivors. The facts, briefly reviewed, are as follows. In 1931, the cabal of the king and the oligarchy who had gambled on dictatorship since 1923 shuffled its ultimate trick: the gradual return to a constitutional government of the old *caciquil* stamp of "bossism." By that time, however, the post-'98 generations had been

[3] Rafael Alberti, *El Poeta en la España de 1931* (Buenos Aires, 1942), pp. 11 and 19. For the autobiography of Alberti, see his *La arboleda perdida* (*Libros I y II de memorias*) (Buenos Aires, 1959), 330 pp., and the "Indice autobiográfico," in his *Poesías completas* (Buenos Aires, 1961), pp. 11–18. For some charming essays on friendships and affinities, see also his *Imagen primera de* . . . (Buenos Aires, 1945), 177 pp.

schooled in a new Spanish temper: a desire for a new Spain in which the situation, good or bad as it might be, could be expected to give rise to a substantially better one. For all the oligarchical pressure for retention of the *status quo*, the dynamism at work in the new forces of the nation could no longer be denied. In the elections of April 12, 1931, and the proclamation of a Spanish Republic on April 14, there was crystallized not merely a change of regime but the transformation of a national way of life that only the armed fist of national and international force could subdue in years to come.

Between 1931–1932, the "honeymoon days" of the Republic, Alberti, under the pensioning hand of the state, studied and traveled in France, Germany, and Russia, in common with old friends and new ones encountered en route—Picasso, Vallejo, Barbusse, Aragon. All, faced with the rising menace of Mussolini and Hitler throughout Europe, turned radical. Back in Spain in 1933, he continued his role of self-styled "poet in the street," and declared himself and his art "at the service of the people." His poetry in these years, or at least a substantial part of it, is aggressive and belligerent in cast. The revolt of the Asturian miners in October, 1934, and its prompt suppression by force, surprised him during the course of further travels abroad, and, delaying his return to a Spain whose government had subverted constitutional justice, he undertook, between poetry and politics, a prolonged tour of the Americas. Back again on the Peninsula in 1936, his civic and militant phase found its deepest engagement in the years of the Popular Front and the Civil War. In common with other poets of Hispanic

INTRODUCTION

loyalties—César Vallejo and Pablo Neruda, for example—or poets writing in other tongues, like Spender, Aragon, and Brecht, he lifted his voice in behalf of an embattled people.

With the collapse of the Republic in 1939, Alberti and his wife took refuge first in France and then in Argentina. There his vocation for painting reasserted itself with all the ardor of a first love. There also his daughter, Aitana, was born and Alberti found a hard peace, always mixed with his nostalgia for his native Spain. In addition to reprinting his previous work, he published in Argentina eight or nine volumes of new poems, in which the urgencies of a decade of civic dedication gradually gave way to a more intimate vein. To mark his sixtieth year Losada published in 1961 his *Poesías completas*, which for all its bulk, is nevertheless already incomplete, in view of the tireless creative thrust of Alberti's genius. In 1964 he took up residence in Italy.

4

It would appear that, with his very first book, Alberti was already a craftsman in total command of his medium, writing with effortless grace and impeccable versification, in brilliant and controlled imagery: a poet at the peak of his form. There is not a false note or a wavering line in the whole of *Marinero en tierra* (1925)—as though, literally born to the art, he was incapable of poetical error. What is admirable, among other things, is the extent to which a youth of limited formal education, appears to have pondered and assimilated the great lyric tradition of his country, the

INTRODUCTION

popular along with the learned. Here was the spectacle of a twenty-two-year-old sufficiently schooled in the poets most admired by a generation before him— Baudelaire, Verlaine, Mallarmé, D'Annunzio, Darío —to profit by their example and supersede it; of a provincial intelligence drenched in the dialect of West Andalusia, commanding a lexicon that would ravish the heart of a purist. It is hardly surprising, under the circumstances, that a jury including two poets of the stature of Machado and Moreno Villa, a dramatic innovator like Arniches, a prose stylist like Miró, and a philologist like Menéndez Pidal should all concur in their appraisal of a first volume by Alberti.

To be sure, there are a number of pieces in *Marinero en tierra* in which Alberti pays his respects to the symbolists; even here, however, the skill with which formulas imported from abroad have been used in the service of personal experience is impressive. Along with his borrowed appurtenances we find, in sharp contrast, a poetical language which leaves symbolism far behind. For even where symbols abound, the Albertian image shows a precision that the symbolists (obsessed with *la nuance, le suggérer*) would never have sanctioned; and metaphorical epithet in the hands of Alberti is as indelibly precise as it is in the classical Spanish tradition. I have in mind, as examples, three sonnets "To Federico García Lorca, poet of Granada" not included in this selection.

All of this brings up the question of the persistence of the traditional in Alberti's poetry as a whole, and its special saliency in his earliest volumes. Part of the charm of *Marinero en tierra* and the two collections that follow it, *La amante* (1925) and *El alba del alhelí*

INTRODUCTION

(1927), is surely our sense of a splendid infusion of the personal inflection of Alberti with elements drawn from the whole fund of the older poetry of Spain—a fusion startling in its blend of the familiar with an element of poetical surprise, of rediscovered delight mixed with pleasures never encountered before. Nothing pleases the Spaniard so much as the shock of the new in the traditional; his gratification is most deeply engaged when powerful factors of identity are rediscovered for him in the present, like portions of his collective and historical continuum. The occasions for such gratification abound in the earlier poems of Alberti. Let me illustrate.

It is by no means unusual to encounter in the traditional ballads of Spain, already in process of compilation in the sixteenth century, a lady who offers herself in the following terms:

Fine horseman, fine gentleman,
carry me off—as your wife,
in the end, if wife you would have,
as your friend, in God's name, if a friend.[4]

Or a third party may appear on the scene to order things thus:

Of three comely sisters
the fairest I give to your hand.
Take her for wife, if wife you would have,
or keep her for friend.[5]

---

[4] *Cancionero de romances impreso en Amberes, sin año, por Martín Nucio*, ed. Ramón Menéndez Pidal (Madrid, 1914), fol. 192v: "Por Dios te ruego caballero / llévesme en tu compañía / si quisieres por mujer / sino sea por amiga." See also fol. 195r.
[5] Julio Cejador y Frauca, *La verdadera poesía castellana* (Madrid, 1921), vol. II, p. 183: "De tres hermanas que tengo / darte he yo la más garrida / si la quieres por mujer / si la quieres por amiga."

INTRODUCTION

Doubtless Alberti had such pieces in mind when he savored their resonance in a poem expressing his own passion for a lady in the present:

As a friend, as a friend,
for friendship's sake only.

As lover, beloved,
for love's sake only.
But never as wife. No.
For friendship's sake only.

(Hacia las tierras altas)

Leafing through the poems of *Marinero en tierra, La amante,* and *El alba del alhelí,* one could compile an impressive repertory of compositions using more or less intact lines, phrases, or paradigms taken from the songbooks of the fifteenth, sixteenth, and seventeenth centuries. It was the purpose of such *cancioneros* and *romanceros* (song and ballad books), in their turn, to collect and preserve examples of that anonymous folk poetry, traditionally a *sung* poetry, whose origins are rooted in the Middle Ages: a poetry of record since the eleventh and twelfth centuries, with elements even earlier in origin, as the study of Mozarabic *jarchyas* (*jarŷas*) in Hispano-Hebraic and Hispano-Arabic literature has shown. It is equally clear that poets of the fifteenth, sixteenth, and seventeenth centuries employed these traditional materials for highly sophisticated ends, turning folk song into art poetry, traditional ballad into art ballad. Lope de Vega, for one, was a consummate master of the genre. And it is the special delight of Alberti in the twentieth century to use analogous materials exactly to the same purpose,

INTRODUCTION

given the fact that the fusion of the traditional and popular with the art poem remains constant in Spanish poetry, and is one of its most salient and distinctive characteristics.

Shall we say, then, that Alberti merely reworked a vein of the traditional verse of his country? Not at all. Rather, his way was to appropriate certain formulas, certain old poems remembered and sung by the people of Spain to this day, or gathered in songbooks which modern scholarship has made accessible, and incorporate them in poems that embody his private sensibility as a poet. Far from being a prisoner of tradition, he has put tradition at the service of the poet, as a tool of individual expression. It is a notion of Alberti's that the old poems had authors now forgotten by the people that sing and perpetuate them; in the course of generations, he explains, repetition has altered the originals, augmenting, deleting, reworking the models with what he happily calls a "kind of memory in motion." [6] In the spirit of this conviction he has taxed himself as a poet to be a part of that memory in motion, bringing to his poems a rhythm, a paradigm, a poetical phrase from the past, modifying them all at will, building them into his medium, aligning himself with a lyric continuum that flows from authors now unknown to the oral revision of poetic materials, and from popular and traditional variants back to the pen of a later individual, in this case, Alberti himself. Since a number of his poems

[6] Rafael Alberti, *La poesía popular en la lírica española* (Jena, 1933), pp. 3 and 20. This notion of Alberti's is a variation on the theories, now confirmed, of Menéndez Pidal on the traditionalism of Spanish poetry.

INTRODUCTION

have been given musical settings, it is far from unlikely that they are being sung in the provinces today by many in complete ignorance of their debt to Rafael Alberti. Indeed, if we are to talk of the "collective unconscious" at all, certainly Alberti is a compelling example of a conscious desire to be a part of the "collective unconscious" of Spanish poetry, national, racial, traditional. If certain of his poems should find their way back to the collective and anonymous tradition of Spain by this means, the feat would constitute considerably more than an accident of personal recognition: it would prove him to be a substantive part of the national sensibility itself.

But the art of Alberti goes beyond the pleasure that comes of recognizing the unprecedented in the patterns and paradigms of precedent, for its effects are precisely the same in poems which make no use whatever of traditional materials. Such is his mastery that he appears to be inviting and refining the past when, in point of fact, he is doing nothing of the sort—when he is *inventing* tradition itself, if the paradox is allowable. An example, "Undersea Street-Cry," will suffice:

How good it would be
to live on a farm in the sea
apart, with a little girl-gardener!

In the smallest of carts, drawn
by a salmon—what delight
to call under sea-salt, love,
a gardener's harvest for all!

"Here's algae! Fresh algae! Get
your algae still wet with the sea!"

INTRODUCTION

Scholars of the future, like scholars confronted today by certain songs of Lope, might well puzzle and bemuse one another with the "problem" of whether such a piece was original with Alberti, or "traditional." They would probably find the poem too "artful" for folk song, in the end, but they would also have to reckon with the fact that, as Machado used to say, nothing is so cultivated in Spain as the popular [7]—that the traditional poetry of Spain is, as often as not, a genre of extraordinary refinement in its rhythmical patterns. It employs precisely the combinations of irregular verse forms [8] and the assonantal octosyllabics that Alberti favors in many of the pieces in his earliest books.

5

It would begin to appear that Alberti is a species now properly classified, like a moth on a pin; but nothing could be further from the truth. As a mobile and sensitive mind and a poet of energetic resources, he proceeded to astonish his readers with two further collections, *Cal y canto* and *Sobre los ángeles*, both published in 1929 and different in manner, feeling, and tone from their predecessors. What helped to bring this about?

In 1924 André Breton had published his first Surrealist Manifesto: in effect, some years after the

[7] Antonio Machado, *Obras completas* (México, 1940), pp. 867–868.
[8] See Pedro Henríquez Ureña, *La versificación irregular en la poesía castellana* (Madrid, 1920), 338 pp.; 2d ed. (Madrid, 1933), 369 pp.

Futurist scandals of Marinetti and the Dadaist nihilism of Tristan Tzara, he came to "organize" (if that is the word) a "system" of irrational poetics, or the poetic exploitation and exploration of the irrational. Having said this much, I should like to go on to insist that the poetry of Alberti is wholly devoid of the irrational and surreal in this sense. It is a fact, however, that the poetry of Europe of that period is permeated with a quality of free association he did not hesitate to employ, on occasion, for his own purposes. The operative words in this case are "employ" and "purposes," rather than "abandon" and "surrender," indispensable to the surrealist mystique.

In 1927, moreover, Spain had celebrated the tercentenary of the death of Góngora with a fresh appreciation of his poetry. The "Gongorist" tradition, calling for a poetry at once sensuous and fastidious, already evident in the work of Darío and Jiménez, was appropriated by Alberti as he had similarly appropriated songbook poetry, not as idle diversion or archaeological reconstruction but as a precision instrument honed and adapted to his own expressive needs.

Put them together: the earlier techniques of Alberti and the later imaginative baroque; the free association of images, and the total mastery of versification, the classical as well as the free; call this a "second manner" of the poet: is it the scope of the complete Alberti? By no means. It is precisely a repertory such as this that makes the poetry of Alberti an inexhaustible venture of distinct and personal mutations.

He might, for example, elect an extreme mode of formality—the Gongoristic and sensuous way of his sonnets, "Araceli," "Amaranta"; he might choose a diversion of sardonic vagaries, deliberately zany in character, turning his whole, immediate world into Chaplinesque horseplay addressed to Harold Lloyd or Buster Keaton; or he might write lyrics in impeccable classical style yet disarmingly modern in theme, like his "Madrigal on A Tram Ticket," handsomely translated by Belitt; he might paint, in powerful images and chiaroscuro, pictures à la Jusepe Ribera, as in "Palco"; or he might trace the inception of ineffable anguish in the flawless quatrains of his "Open Letter," translated in kind in this volume:

And what of my soul? How long has it been
since it broke all the records for absence and won
all the marathon prizes? What to do with a heart, between
　　chance
and disaster—taunted by one or the other, yet numb in
　　the middle?

Finally, impatient with each of his masks, he might, as in *Sobre los ángeles*, draw on all the forms, classical and free, on logic and incoherence, reason and free association, to investigate the ascents and descents of good and bad angels coexisting in the devastated psyche of man.

Sobre los ángeles is a book in the tragic mode. The paradisal security and poise previously radiated by Alberti—his characteristic gusto for life, love, and reality—succumbed, in his twenty-fifth year, to a spiritual crisis. Something seminal and grave broke in the depths of his being, as it appears to have broken in other poets of his epoch—the Vallejo of *Trilce*

(1922), the Neruda of *Residencia en la tierra* (1925–1935), the Lorca of *Poeta en Nueva York* (1929), the Eliot of *The Wasteland* (1921–1922)—all poets of a disintegrating world, a world dissolving under their gaze into a species of modern death dance, a world in which matter and mankind seemed equally undone. "Shape without form, shade without colour, / Paralysed force, gesture without motion," as Eliot lamented in "The Hollow Men" (1925).[9] Alberti's case is all the more tragic in that it forces to the breaking point a previously unflawed belief in an ebullient and charming reality reflected in his earliest poetry. It is no exaggeration to say that Alberti suffered a double ordeal in the poems of this period: a crisis of delayed adolescence and a crisis of consciousness from which he emerged, no longer the youth of Cádiz but a man at large in the world, having forfeited the innocent delights of his childhood and youth but aware, as never before, of a complex reality, compelling both his confrontation and his understanding.

From the very first page of *Sobre los ángeles*, Alberti formulates the problem with his customary precision:

Where is that Paradise,
shadow, lately your home?
Ask it in stillness.

Unanswering cities,
mute rivers, peaks
of no echo, inarticulate seas.

Nobody knows. . . .

[9] T. S. Eliot, *The Complete Poems and Plays, 1909–1950* (New York: Harcourt, Brace, 1952), p. 56.

INTRODUCTION

Thus Alberti, who had previously set himself the Orphic task of interpreting the speech of oceans and mountains, rivers and cities, now finds them silent, uninhabited, mute. That paradise where all was once mathematically clear, peopled with "Virgins with T-squares / and compasses, tending / the heavenly blackboards," and with "Angels of number, / musing and flying / out of 1 into 2, out of 2 / into 3, out of 3 into 4," now appears to him hidden in the mists:

Neither crescent nor star, sun
or the thunderclap's
green, or the air,
or the bolt in the air. Only mists.

Virgins empty of T-squares
and compasses, weeping.

And there on the carrion slates,
the angel of number,
a corpse in the mummy-cloth,
aloft on the 1 and the 2,
on the 3 and the 4 . . .

In terror and distress he declares himself lost:

I search in the death
of my hopes for a portico's
green in the blackened abysses.
. . . .
Away! Away with them all! What
unspeakable panic of shadows!
What collapses of spirit!

However, in the quest for illumination and grace which brought him to the verge of those "blackened abysses," Alberti was not one to submit without a

INTRODUCTION

life-and-death struggle, even when, as his poems make clear, his adversaries would not reveal themselves or disclose the nature of his struggle; when, in his own image, his ordeal was compounded of "wind against wind / and I, in the middle, / a tower undefended."

Nevertheless, in a new "invitation to the harp" of the bardic vocation, he could still invoke a new vision of his world, he could still hew a path, however buffeted by contradictory winds, to a hard-won redemption. Taking counsel with himself, he had grasped the main fact: that the pursued must always press forward, must move into his peril and then beyond it, to whatever he was fated to confront; that his pain and his punishment were cosmic, as well as personal—a purgatorial phase, it might be, on the way to a later paradise. The journey, he sensed, led on:

Distantly, distantly.
. . . .
Ever and always more distantly.
Where the pith of the wood keeps the echo and print of
    our passage,
where the moth wakes a hush of cravats,
and a century's length is a harp left abandoned.

Thus, in a lost world, the poet's quest was always *plus ultra*, toward a new day, another dawn. For if *Sobre los ángeles* is tragic in its inflection, it is not, in its total impact, despairing. Throughout the whole of the book—and it may be *because* of it—Alberti toils from a position of tragic despair, through the stations of a tragic encounter, to tragic ascendency.

What should not escape our considered attention is that Alberti, in the midst of stark spiritual and emotional stress, of human and cosmic anguish, has exquisitely dominated his medium. The "lost" who maintain order and balance in the midst of spiritual chaos surely are never irretrievably lost. In *Sobre los ángeles*, the passion for poetical order takes a number of guises. It reveals itself in the metrical constructions of the trimmed line, a gift of his earlier prosody; it spins out a long line without meter or rhyme, but charged with an emotional rhythm that pulsates with the heartbeat of animate anguish that analyzes as it suffers. Thus, the Alberti of *Sobre los ángeles* simultaneously enacts a double identity, a twofold ordeal: that of the patient on the analyst's couch, babbling his intimate panic, and the analyst at his side who listens, observes, and interprets.

6

More than any other book, it is this book that marks the decisive crisis in the life and the art of Alberti. Thereafter, especially from 1929 to 1935, other poems are more somberly reflective, like those on the death of Fernando Villalón and Ignacio Sánchez Mejías, for example. Others bid constant farewell to all he has put behind him, with titles like "Farewell to Lost Light," "They Have Gone," "Nothing More Can Avail." A large number of poems, as it happens, are cast in free verse; but little by little, his reorganization of a later vision of the world returns to the classical meters, even when overflowing with the fluid obscurity of darkness and blood of his newly discovered "tragic sense of life."

An intricate example of his work of this era is *Verte y no verte* (1935), his elegy on Ignacio Sánchez

INTRODUCTION

Mejías, a bullfighter of exceptional heart and intellect, a friend of ballerinas and writers, poets and folk singers, killed by a *toro bravo*. The elegy is composed of four sonnets alternating with short-line songs and poems of free verse. Each of the four sonnets sings of the "bull of death," armed equally with horns and an annihilative destiny, fated to "live armed with a shadow, and challenge an armor of light." Savagery confronts valor, both worthy foemen, and beast and man meet in the rites of their dying. The sonnets, all in perfect hendecasyllabic lines, with the ABBA ABBA CDE CDE rhyme scheme preferred by Garcilaso, Herrera, and Góngora and similarly classic in profile, are charged with oracular feeling in their verbal execution, keyed to the premonitory images of prophetical discourse—the language of the Sibyl, but by no means Delphic in effect. For example, Sonnet 2, addressed to the "bull of death," alludes to a *toro bravo* obviously native to the marshlands of Cádiz—one of those bulls encountered by Alberti in his Andalusian adolescence when, as the Spanish goes, "playing the maverick" (*hacer novillos*, "playing hooky") he joined other young vagrants to take his turn at the *muleta*—in short, a well-blooded bull whose instincts might bring him to charge at the surf line itself:

He with the rapier who whets your nostalgias—
your dream of the gout in the thigh and gangrene—
not even the herdsman can bring you to heel.

Charge at the sea, bull, charge and strike home in your
    rage.
Ride down the killer of spindrift in the brine and the sand,
whom nothing can save, and deal him the death that you
    willed.

INTRODUCTION

The short-line songs, in their turn, evoke the voyaging of the poet, literally en route from Spain to distant ports, and the progressive alienation of the bullfighter, afloat on the ship of his death. The free verse pieces have still another function: to embody the poet's reflections not only on the unique death that he elegizes, but also on death as such, ineluctable and fatal, exacting each man's confrontation, as with Sánchez Mejías. Finally, with the acceptance of man's human and mortal condition, we have the upsurge of the concluding strophe, for the most part in somber, Dantesque tercets, in which the death and the life of Ignacio, in Alberti's words, are "joined in my veins and made whole / in my solitude and survive from within." For the poet, the measure is a lifetime; for his readers and for posterity, it is the lifetime of a poem.

It must not be forgotten, as I have already indicated, that the political and social consciousness of Alberti was also unfolding its vision at this time. He had found, or so it seemed to Alberti, a philosophical basis for being, in his dedication to a doctrine which promised a better life—perhaps a new paradise to replace Paradise Lost—here on earth as he knew it. Alberti is not the only poet whose faith was to take such a turn and muster his art and being "under new flags," as Pablo Neruda sang. He openly professed his new allegiance when, in the 1934 edition of his poems written between 1924 and 1930, he declared them a "cycle now closed." [10] In effect, from that time to 1940, the major portion of his poetry is "implemental" in character: a "third manner," political in theme and

[10] Rafael Alberti, *Poesías, 1924–1930* (Madrid, 1934), p. 25.

implication. It is worth noting, however, that his poetry in this vein remains poetry above all, whatever adjective we summon to qualify it. Its range is epic or elegiac at will, far removed from the crass propaganda of others. Its high points are aptly suggested in the four poems chosen by Ben Belitt from many others drawing their inspiration from the cause of the Spanish Republic in the anguish and glory of its Civil War years.

Later, in exile, Alberti used as the epigraph of his first American volume of poems, *Entre el clavel y la espada* (1941), another poem written in Madrid during the war years. Here, with characteristic sagacity, he anticipates all that his poetry might yet come to be—had, in fact, then come to be—in more tranquil times:

After this willful derangement, this harassed
and necessitous grammar by whose haste I must live,
let the virginal word come back to me whole and meticulous,
and the virginal verb, justly placed with its rigorous adjective.

While it qualifies meadow and mountain to speak of their green,
or invokes all the sky, repeating its blue to the ocean:
let the whole heart be moved to its depths, as though all had not been,
and the tongue in my mouth touch the awe of unwritten creation.

What Alberti foresaw in the quatrains quoted above was a resurgence of imaginative peace for a new world

INTRODUCTION

newly born out of war, in which he could create in a new chastity of spirit; but the new world for whose birth he had fought in Spain was tragically aborted. By 1939, the forces of darkness had overpowered the forces of light; and in his Argentine refuge, Alberti was obsessively tormented by the spectacle of Spain's martyrdom, at the same time that he began to rediscover, in Andean Córdoba, the intactness of the natural world—objects and men restored to harmonious form, delivered from the physical and spiritual violence wreaked on his suffering country. His first Argentine poems read like a veritable elegy for Spain: "Let me weep like a river / enormously weep like a torrent"; or:

Fallen! O fallen!
the children of light in the broken cities
where the gradual dawns taste of death
and the yelping dogs run wild in a desolation . . .

However, the poems are equally striking for their reassertion of the integrity of the natural world, elemental and incorruptible:

The very cobbles leap up: out of the clay of its entrails,
resins unload, wellsprings, the green of the poplars.
All trembles and crackles, strains forward, lashes out, and
    explodes.
Life cleaves to life, splits asunder to magnify life.
And however death forces its forfeits or gains its advantage,
the fields lie before us for battle, and the battle is
    jubilant.

7

Another sign of the resurgence of the life-force was given the Albertis in the birth of their daughter, Aitana, in Buenos Aires in 1941. A new aura of hope illumines his next book, *Pleamar* (1944). The elegies and requiems always present in his later work yield the place of honor to lullabies and lyrics which, in effect, interpret the world to his daughter and his daughter to the world:

For you, child, Aitana,
restoring the rivers,
this bough of sweet water.

The sweets of the water, little bough,
little daughter, lest the salt find you.
The well in the sugar, great bough,
little branch, that never grows bitter.

Restoring the rivers . . .

In this spirit of renewal, a refreshed Alberti came once more to feel the old pleasure in line and in form, the excitements of drawing and painting. To this rekindling delight, implemented by his own labors as an artist, he dedicated the whole of his *A la pintura* (1948). The collection is an extraordinary one, recalling the poems addressed to painting, architecture, music, printing, and the rest, of the Age of Enlightenment. But Alberti's homage shows more than illustrative intelligence: there is an intensity and passion wholly lacking in the didactic set pieces of the eighteenth century. Alberti sings the arts of painting in a variety of styles fitted, with infallible poetical flair, to

INTRODUCTION

the special idiosyncracies of his theme. Precise, mathematical sonnets are devoted to plastic and graphic principles, to the theories of the physical components of painting (the retina, the hand, the palette, the brush, the canvas) or to structural aspects of line, perspective, composition, proportion, color, and light. There is a witty adaptation of the form of each longer poem to the style of the eulogized painter: lauds in honor of the medieval Giotto, open compositions in free verse for a contemporary like Picasso, and veritable fugues in praise of all the colors of the spectrum. The juxtaposition of poems is similarly programmatic: a sonnet to mural painting, for example, accompanies poems to Michelangelo and Raphael; a sonnet to chiaroscuro precedes a poem dedicated to Rembrandt; another addressed to drapery sets off a song for Zurbarán; a sonnet to light parallels his homage for Velázquez, just as a poem on the color black serves to incise poems to Valdés Leal and Goya. One discovers that the Italianate preferences of Alberti range from Giotto to Veronese, and his Spanish predilections encompass the centuries from Berruguete to Goya. Significantly, only two moderns are included in the book: Gutiérrez Solana and Picasso. There is also a marked preference for figurative art, and for concepts of order, proportion, and geometrical beauty, in the "theoretical" pieces. The "rage for order" that distinguishes Alberti from the outset, and toward which even the panic of *Sobre los ángeles* gropes, is equally apparent in his visual taste. A *la pintura*, in the end, is yet another celebration of the imaginative ordering of reality.

INTRODUCTION

Consonant with his zest for the real, Alberti does not now disclaim his former involvement in the sociopolitical life of his era. In his *Coplas de Juan Panadero* (1949–1953), his sequences on Poland, Russia, and China (1958), and innumerable other pieces in his recent collections, the voice of the artist engaged in the contentions of his time demands to be heard. But the dominant sentiment of his poetry during the course of the last decade and a half has been an obsessive nostalgia for his country, for erotic fulfillment, the amenities of friendship and art, and the passion for nature.

His volume of 1953, *Ora Maritima*, an homage to the trimillenium of Cádiz, is an example of his poetry of nostalgia for his homeland. It draws, in part, on the account of a voyage around the coast of southern Spain six centuries before Christ, as it was retold in the fourth century of our era in a Latin poem by Ruphus Festus Avienus (the same poem from which Alberti has taken his title), and on a variety of classical sources, both Latin and Greek, bearing on the mythology of Cádiz. Here again, the poet, as in his very earliest books, has saturated himself in a flowing Hispanic continuum that streams from the dawn of historical time to the present. If, for example, in a charming ballad reminiscent of seventeenth-century art ballads on Greek themes, it suits Alberti to rehearse one of the twelve labors of Hercules—the death of Geryon and the theft of his bulls from the pastures near Andalusian Tartessos—he is present in modern as well as mythical time. He is aware that other fierce bulls cropping the grasses of Cádiz have been harried and hauled away to their doom since the time of the mythical grandson of Ocean, monarch, god, and "steward of the bulls of the marshlands." Again, the accomplishment of Alberti is not to be dismissed as mere archaeological divertissement, but offers further proof of his genius for fusing personal experience and the memory of his country with remotest mythology.

A slightly earlier collection, *Retornos de lo vivo lejano* (1952)—largely devoted to odes in classical meters—shows Alberti, seasoned in exile and the melancholy of passing years, still preoccupied with love in its many guises: love of wife, of daughter, friends, Spain, nature, justice, art, and the total compass of living. The inflection is more considered, perhaps, but the effect is no less volatile, ardent, and consummate than that of his youth. A further work, *Baladas y canciones del Paraná* (1953–1954), also looks back with deepening nostalgia to the country of his youth and young manhood, in the style of the "Song 8" and the "Ballad of the Lost Andalusian" here translated by Belitt. Here, too, in the midst of homesickness and the cherished remembrance of past friends, the bursts of illumination persist:

You shall gather the best
of that beauty into your hand.
On that day of all days you shall see it
and rest.

8

The day and the vision of accomplished repose, it would seem, have not yet been given into the hand of Rafael Alberti. He goes on with the tasks appointed to him as a poet: survival and song. His poetry continues its labor of purifying for all our sense of ourselves, interpreting ourselves to ourselves, in the inchoate music of our times. His is the triumph of the largest of talents that bear self-knowledge to all, toiling "without haste and without pause, like the stars."

Luis Monguió

*University of California,
Berkeley*

TRANSLATOR'S PREFACE

If a "selected Alberti" implies an obligation to embrace the whole accomplishment of a poet, choose at will among the pieces assembled, and find the wit and the English to translate accordingly, this is not a "selected poems" of Rafael Alberti. I cannot pretend, for example, that I have chosen to exclude from this anthology that small sunburst of graces which makes the earliest volume of Alberti, *Marinero en tierra* (1925) and the volumes which follow it in 1925 (*La amante*) and 1927 (*El alba del alhelí*) so irresistible. The *coplas, madrigales,* and *pregones* go by default, rather than by choice: after years of trying to turn them into *faits* of translation, I have had to conclude, a little sullenly, they are paradisal soufflés whose chemical nature it was to rise only once. As Ricardo Gullon [1] has pointed out, "they appear to be pure emanations, transcending all effort"; they hover like spray on the wave of that childhood when, in Alberti's words, "my eyes were giddy with quicklime, packed with white salt from the estuaries, pierced by the blues and pure yellows, the violets and greens of my river, my ocean, my beaches, and pines."

For all their disarming immediacy, however—the effect of which is to suspend meditation and enchant

[1] Alegrías y sombras de Rafael Alberti," *Insula*, no. 198 (Madrid, May, 1963).

TRANSLATOR'S PREFACE

with facts of pure pleasure—a touch of English reveals them to be artifacts of the poet's vocation, complex systems of rhythm, vagary, and refrain set into place with implacable virtuosity. One discovers, in an apparently airy "confection" from the *Marinero*, that all is irreducibly *substantive*, wrought into the time and the temper of the Andalusian "sound" as the wreath is wrought into the steel in the damascene art of Toledo. Rhythm for rhythm and word after word, they accomplish continuing miracles of utterance innate to the syntax and brio of the Spanish. The word falls where it wills, infallible, unforced, providential; and behind it, the whole balladic tradition of Spain is at work in its combination of the artful and the popular, investing the song of Alberti with pressures that pull at the depths of a language—specifically, the Spanish language—like the pull of a tide. They are intransmissible.

My defection is not helped by the fact that *Marinero en tierra* won for the poet of twenty-two the Premio Nacional de Literatura (1925), the nod of Antonio Machado and Menéndez Pidal, among other judges, and the thorny cordiality of Juan Ramón Jiménez, whose sponsoring letter introduces the poems with a seignorial expectation of fealty to come. Having confessed the partial failure of an intention, however, I should like to point out that, in all other respects, I believe this representation from the *Poesías completas* to be an actively "selective" one: some fifty poems from eleven volumes written over an interval of thirty years, with the emphasis bearing strongly on *Sobre los ángeles,* V*erte y no verte,* A *la pintura,* and the

TRANSLATOR'S PREFACE

Retornos de lo vivo lejano—the gamut of Alberti as Gongorist, agonist, elegist, "poet in the street," painter, and exile.

The result, to be sure, is an Alberti *en tierra*, a land-locked Alberti: and an Alberti *en tierra* is primarily a poet of exile, a "lost Andalusian" whose dominant themes are bereavement, banishment, and nostalgia: *"arboledas perdidas"* (vanished groves), *"paraísos perdidos"* (lost paradises), *"retornos"* (returns), *"sombras malditas"* (accursed shadows), *"toros de la muerte"* (bulls of death) and similar phantasms of expatriation. His orbit is purgatorial rather than paradisal: a limbo presided over by an inchoate pantheon of angels, tubercular nightmares, neurasthenia, civil war, Keystone comedians, the mystique of the bullring and the demigods of the Prado, and the muse of intimate memory.

Doubtless, for the reader of Alberti accustomed to the indigo-and-aquamarine world of his "land-sailor," the picture demands a sobering reversal of perspective. C. M. Bowra[2] was among the first to emphasize the primacy of a "crisis of an imaginative spirit" concerned with "dark movements and situations of the soul," and to weigh the angelism of Alberti against the bicarbonated jubilation of his seascapes, his sailor blouses, Andalusian whitewashes, and that gift of balladic timing for which there is no word but *gracia*. As early as 1937, moreover, Dudley Fitts, whose eye for the depths and surfaces of literatures, past and present, provincial and exotic, is virtually infallible, introduced

[2] C. M. Bowra, *The Creative Experiment* (New York: Grove Press, 1958), vii, "Rafael Alberti, *Sobre los ángeles*."

his *Poems (1929–1936)* [3] with a mordant epigraph from Alberti (*"Para ir al infierno, no hace falta cambiar de sitio ni postura:* To go to hell, one need never change place or position"). Fitts chose as first poem in the collection his "Homage to Rafael Alberti":

Rafael, in your Cádiz, white against blue quadrate
In your District of Angels, Cádiz,
If there is cadence of wind or sun, bells
Toll it, record it; and you
Translate the liquid characters as they run
The shudder of rain on the roofs is rain only,
Rain, rain only; but within the rain your Angels—
Informing rain and roofs and the stippled entries,
The wine-shop cats crouched in the sweet dust of wine,
Shell, wire, langosta, razorblade, musty files—
Move hugely, quiet; and your stricken eyes
Mark the santoral-sinew pulsing there,
Throbbing,
            Angel-rain, Angel-world, meaning-of-Angels,
              Ladder of Cádiz, hallow-of-Angels-latent,
The delicate armies, inward fire white
Alleluyas of glass and bell, forever bright.

The selection of this book is weighted in the spirit of that mood. Between the angels and sailors of Alberti's youth, and the melancholia of later works like the *Retornos de lo vivo lejano* (1952) and *Baladas y canciones del Paraná* (1953–1954), lies a lifetime of displacement and homesickness elegized in prose, in nostalgic detail, in an intimate *recherche du temps perdu*,[4] (*La arboleda perdida* / A Vanished Grove)

---

[3] Dudley Fitts, *Poems (1929–1936)* (Norfolk, Conn.: New Directions, 1937).

complete to the Proustian adjective: *perdu*. Here, the lost, the banished, the repudiated—"*lo perdido*," "*lo lejano*"—emerge as obsessional themes of a postwar Alberti, just as the increasing formalization of his prosody reflects the pressures of exile and longing that drive "a rainy evening," "a birthday," "an abandoned museum," Chopin, and "love in a theater loge" through fastidious spirals of syntax and bereavement, like the humming in a shell. The reader in quest of the "complete" Alberti can never forget that, for all his earlier scintillation, the "quicklime and song" of his baroque and flamenco phases, his dominant signature is elegiac and his vocation, mourning.

It is my hope that these selections, with the accompanying excerpts from *A Vanished Grove*, will reflect the refinement and persistence of that motif, which is a "persistence of memory" not as di Chirico or Dalí, the friend of his youth, imagined it, magically distorted by mannequins, optical illusions, and the special lighting that turns even pebbles monstrous, but exactly as last encountered by the poet. In that world of total recall (*retornos*), all has been stopped as in a fairy story: "the delectable book fallen limp on the floor," the "currants and strawberries" in their "hidden recess," García Lorca in the "glaze of expensive alpaca as though recently turned by the shears," the "drench of immediate blues, wet blue over blues," "tablecloths on a table," the "abrupt or the gradual / running of wines," "pieces and clutter—Heaven knows what they mean." All is remembered with a grieving insistence

[4] *La arboleda perdida*, Libros I y II (Buenos Aires: Compañía General Fabril Editora, 1959).

upon family, *tierra,* and a long anguish of exile that, at its best, calls to mind the *Poemas humanos* of another casualty of expatriation, César Vallejo.

As to the mode of my translation, I have the customary misgivings and satisfactions, plus the edgy knowledge that in my search for equivalent outcomes, I have often been forced further from the literal than I would wish to go, **kept** there by the pulse I have placed under my English to give it character and "closure," and left with only a wet forefinger to measure which way the winds of equivalence were blowing. It was my conviction, for example, that the sonnets and tercets of Alberti, in which, as in Góngora, all is "resilient, transparent, and colorless," stored "in cut-crystal, in caskets and urns," must be confronted as such, rather than reduced to denotative puddings or lumps of invertebrate English. What to do, moreover, with a "flat" line from *"Carta abierta":*

Roma y Cartago frente a frente iban

literally rendered, "Rome and Carthage went face to face" (if not, indeed, forehead to forehead), but actually intending the work teams into which classrooms were competitively divided in provincial Jesuit schools, "Romans and Carthaginians," much as Joyce invoked them in his *Portrait* as "Lancaster and York"? Or the "castillos"

del Pím-Pám-Púm de los tres Reyes Magos

in the *"Guía estival del paraíso,"* literally and inscrutably the "castles of Pim-Pam-Pum of the Three

TRANSLATOR'S PREFACE

Magi," but intending a child's shooting gallery (Pím-Pám-Púm) where rubber balls serve in place of bullets or pellets, recalled in an overlay of Christmas festivity? Or the climactic groan of the elegist in V*erte y no verte:*

Había olvidado ahora que le hablaba de usted no de tú,
    desde siempre

literally "I had forgotten now I have been speaking to you as *usted* [formal address] not as *tú* [intimate address] all along." Or the unabashed churrigueresqueries of *"El niño de la Palma," "Goya,"* or *"Gutiérrez Solana":*

Lo mas pálido
ético
perlético
perlipelambrético . . .
lo mas goyesco
quevedesco
valle-inclanesco
del cuesco.

Indeed, there is good reason to question whether any language that issues from the art and the hammer of the poem can be neutrally approached or remain "literal." The fact of placement, of long marination in the tension and time of the poet's experience, the vatic thrust that commits it from the unforeseeable, to the shaping *poiesis* that sustains and astonishes the poet in the end, preempt "literal" outcomes. Precisely to the extent that a poem is never *foresayable,* and that paraphrase, criticism, and elucidation remove themselves from the afflatus that imagined the parts, and deal only with the *said*, it repels "literal" reduction. Even the notion that a poem, once composed, is a *terminal* datum is an imaginative rather than a literal one; nor do we need Valéry to remind us that poems are not terminated but abandoned.

Semantically, the "terminal fallacy" leads to the further illusion that the *words* in the poem are terminal, as words in a dictionary are thought to be so, and must be treated accordingly by the translator. The final vulgarity is the assumption that translation must take teachable form, in the end, and subserve, like a lever or a plasterer's hod, the contrivances of the classroom and the tactical labors of the grammarian. On the contrary, the whole ambience of poetry suggests that translations, like all other things that tax us with the *whole* force of their character, are literal only by expedience, and that their literalness tells us nothing at all about *poetry*. The leaf of grass that Whitman raised to his eye with the poet's cry: "What is grass?" and the poem that embodies that cry are equally tentative encounters in the history of perception; and the translator must invest each with corresponding enactments of being.

This I have tried to accomplish in the translations here assembled, with varying proximity to the original. Not all will thank me for my labors; and yet, to bring *whole* poems into my "frequency" as a translator and cope simultaneously with substantive, prosodic, and textural considerations which in the end deliver a poet *alive*, nothing less will serve. On the whole, my English translation has aimed at a line-for-line correspondence of format, except for the indentation of first lines,

TRANSLATOR'S PREFACE

where I have departed from Spanish printing procedures, to suggest the contrast of traditional Spanish meters with the rhythms available in English. For those who wish to have their cake and eat it too—the usurers and bookkeepers of translation, and the sages who see the One True Translation in the middle of the air, like Ezekiel's wheel—the curve of deviation will appear perilous. It has seemed so to me, on occasion: yet I hope that the total venture of this volume will make the difference between a persistently untranslated Alberti, and an Alberti who may now begin to take shape in "selective" form and suggest the range of his accomplishment as a poet.

These remarks are quizzically and not controversially intended. They should not, for example, distract the reader from his scrutiny of the essential datum of this translation: the mind and the art and the vision of a poet already written deeply into the grain of contemporary letters and the genius of his country. We tend to look away too long from the fruits of translation, such as they are, to the theorist's concern for the criteria of translation, on the assumption that translation will wait until the issues, which are bottomless, have been resolved by an ecumenical council of pundits. But next to the community of scholars, the community of translators is perhaps the most savage and anthropophagous of the species. One will contend that an English Neruda ought not to sound as if the translator was "writing like Shakespeare," when everyone knows Neruda should sound like a pirate. Another will invoke anonymity, piously disavowing alternatives never his to enact in the first place, and, for the best

TRANSLATOR'S PREFACE

reasons in the world, lay a dead mouse at the feet of the master. Another, in the interests of "the poem itself," will follow one volume of Pushkin with three of himself, in an exegetical dazzle, like a competing soprano, in which all that was lost to the "literal" is pure *bel canto* for the critic. To each his own; I applaud the heterogeneous way; ours is a comic vocation.

My acknowledgments are simple and massive. They relate wholly to the patience of Dr. Luis Monguió, of the Department of Spanish and Portuguese of the University of California, who proposed a "selected Alberti" in bilingual form, held me to the task when I was prepared to abandon it, plied me with counsel and suggestion between one draft and another, for which I am happily indebted, and furnished an Introduction, for which readers in English are equally in debt. Without that buoyant and exacting intelligence, watchful for the truth of the poet and the truths of translation, this volume would not have been possible. Finally, I must thank the editors of *Poetry, The Southern Review, The Quarterly Review of Literature,* and *The Sewanee Review* for permission to reprint translations which first appeared in their pages, and in one instance, for a prose "Note on the Later Alberti" incorporated into this preface.

BEN BELITT

Bennington College

RAFAEL ALBERTI
SELECTED POEMS

A Vanished Grove: 1

All excerpts grouped under this title are from Alberti's autobiography-in-progress, of which two books were published by 1959 under the title *La arboleda perdida*, covering the years 1902–1931.

My childhood in Puerto de Santa María was shaped and enriched by a gamut of azure. I have sounded it over and over in the songs of my first books: they are hoarse with its overtones . . . Between the blues of aprons and pinafores, sailor blouses, skies, the river, the bay, and the island, boats, breezes, I opened my eyes and I learned how to read. When the letters first joined into words, or the words linked and chimed to envision my feelings, I cannot say precisely. After many sullen labors and vigils, surely, many tears in the corner, many sad suppers dessertless to bed . . . On the hard day of the miracle, my eyes opened wide on a book, forced all the power of my blood to my tongue, made it give back, as though strung on a cable that might suddenly wrench into bits, the following dizzying paragraph:

> *The soldiers went forth into battle and marched nine hours without sleep . . .*

Most prodigious hour of them all, incredible day when silence broke into sound, syllables streamed on the wind, fused into words, rolled through the valleys and hills in hymns from the sea that exploded in bubbles and sand! Yet that very same evening a child wept and knew nothing: he dreamed in big-bellied letters that pursued him like giants, lunged at him heavily, to trap and encircle him,

A VANISHED GROVE: 1

backed him into cobwebby corners grubby and gray as a capital letter, gave him no quarter. The next day, too grown-up to wet his bed any longer, our schoolboy looks up at his mama and is properly chided and punished . . .

From the schoolhouses of Andalusia, both primary and secondary, one emerged crazy with prayers and a head full of horrendous sermons, having shored up a junkpile of orthographical failings and follies so immense that even at twenty, after five years in Madrid, I blushed at the all-encompassing wit of a moppet of eleven enrolled at the Instituto Escuela, or some such pedagogical haven. Unlucky generations of Spain, spawned in such putrefaction, incubated in the dens of such filthy banality! . . . What agonized arms, what breasts struggling in pride and despair to surmount all that emptiness, have we witnessed together, without one glint of sun in the end? What a ruin of families! Detestable heirloom of shipwrecks and garbage! The best-loved friends of my childhood and youth, afloat on those middens of desolate cinder, lost beyond hope of my ever seeing them firm in the sunlight, restored. There come tossing, on seas of deprival, like drowners alive, my sisters and brothers and cousins, a whole clutter of casual school friends—worst of all, honored teachers schooled in a more literate dispensation . . .

In the tercentenary year of D. Luis de Góngora, my passion for verbal refinement in poetry reached its apogee: the formalization of the beautiful, in *Quicklime and Song*, overmastered me, almost to the point of petrifying feeling entirely . . . This was painterly poetry—plastic, linear, profiled, confined. All the brio and flair of my earlier songs I stored, as in cut-crystal, in caskets and urns where all was resilient, transparent, and colorless. I subjected my metrical line to the utmost precision and pressure. I toiled, like one possessed, for pure beauty of idiom, the most tensile of

A VANISHED GROVE: 1

harmonies, timbres, sending image after image in a series, in the course of a single poem, with cinematographic velocity; for it was the cinema, above all other inventions of modern life, that charmed and engaged me the most. In the motion picture, I felt, new dimensions of vision had sprung into life, new modes of feeling had toppled, almost at a touch, the old order of things already crumbling in the ruin of World War I. Breaking free for a moment from my tercets and sonnets and the calculated Gongorism of my manner, I asserted with jubilant conviction:

> *I was born—take my word for it—in the Sign of the Cinema,*
> *under crisscrossing planes, among reels of electrical cable,*
> *when all the King's coaches were turned into obsolete fables,*
> *and even the Pope rode to work via automobile.*

CAL Y CANTO
QUICKLIME AND SONG

(1929)

Cal y canto is also the mason's stock phrase for quicklime and rock, or building stone. The ambiguity of the Spanish noun, *canto* (rock, stone, and song) has no equivalence in English, and forces a choice from the translator not present in the original.—B. B.

Carta Abierta
(*Falta el primer pliego*)

... Hay peces que se bañan en la arena
y ciclistas que corren por las olas.
Yo pienso en mí. Colegio sobre el mar.
Infancia ya en balandro o bicicleta.

    Globo libre, el primer balón flotaba
sobre el grito espiral de los vapores.
Roma y Cartago frente a frente iban,
marineras fugaces sus sandalias.

    Nadie bebe latín a los diez años.
El Álgebra, ¡quién sabe lo que era!
La Física y la Química, ¡Dios mío,
si ya el sol se cazaba en hidroplano!

    ... Y el cine al aire libre. Ana Bolena,
no sé por qué, de azul, va por la playa.
Si el mar no la descubre, un policía
la disuelve en la flor de su linterna.

    Bandoleros de smoking, a mis ojos
sus pistolas apuntan. Detenidos,
por ciudades de cielos instantáneos,
me los llevan sin alma, vista sólo.

    Nueva York está en Cádiz o en el Puerto.
Sevilla está en París, Islandia o Persia.
Un chino no es un chino. Un transeúnte
puede ser blanco al par que verde y negro.

Open Letter
(*First Page Missing*)

        . . . Fish swim in the sand
and cyclists are skimming the waves:
which gives one to ponder: my schooldays afloat on the
    sea,
my salad days, rocking a boat or riding a bicycle.

The first balloon going up, a world without strings,
on the circular hoot of a pleasure-boat, a spiral of steam.
"Carthage and Rome" at their wars, all the classroom
contenders, or sea-going truants, footloose on the beach in
    their sandals.

Who laps up his Latin declensions at ten?
And algebra, chemistry, physics—good Lord, who could
care, who could reckon it up in his head, in a world
where men tracked down the sun in a seaplane, they said!

In the open-air movies, Anne Boleyn
on the beach, wearing blue for no manifest reason: if
the tide doesn't get to her first, the police
will turn on the flower of their flashlights and finish her off.

There are gangsters in dinner coats, with pistol points
aimed at my eyes . . . They are booked for arrest
and are known to be desperate . . . They move out of
    range as I look,
swept away, city by city, lost in immediate sky.

New York or Cádiz, Cádiz or El Puerto,
Paris or Iceland, Persia, Seville. All's not Chinese
that appears so: black is white, if the bypasser wills,
and black or white is no better than green.

En todas partes, tú, desde tu rosa,
desde tu centro inmóvil, sin billete,
muda la lengua, riges rey de todo...
Y es que el mundo es un álbum de postales.

Multiplicado pasas en los vientos,
en la fuga del tren y los tranvías.
No en ti muere el relámpago que piensas,
sino a un millón de lunas de tus labios.

Yo nací —¡respetadme!— con el cine.
Bajo una red de cables y aviones.
Cuando abolidas fueron las carrozas
de los reyes y al auto subió el Papa.

Vi los telefonemas que llovían,
plumas de ángel azul, desde los cielos.
Las orquestas seráficas del aire
guardó el auricular en mis oídos.

De lona y níquel, peces de las nubes
bajan al mar periódicos y cartas.
(Los carteros no creen en las sirenas
ni en el vals de las olas, sí en la muerte.

And so you are everywhere:
You are there and you stalk from your rose's immovable
    center, without
even the price of a ticket, tongue-tied and cock-of-the
    walk . . .
The world is your keepsake, postcards in a photograph
    album.

Repeated, you coast on the wind, you come and you go
on a flying express, or the tracks of a tram.
The bolt that you tense in your mind will never quite
    fizzle,
but wane on the tip of your tongue, like a moon, a million
    moons hence.

I was born—take my word for it!—in the Sign of the
    Cinema,
under crisscrossing planes, among reels of electrical cable,
when all the king's coaches were turned into obsolete
    fables
and even the Pope rode to work via automobile.

I saw long-distance telephone messages drop from the
    clouds,
angelically blue in their envelopes, a downpour of feathers;
philharmonic recitals with seraphs performing in air;
and I listened with earphones and receivers glued to my
    ears.

Aerial fish falling, newspapers and letters
in oceans of canvas and nickel. (Postmen today are so
    skeptical:
they think only of death while the Lorelei sing
from the rocks, and have nothing whatever to say for the
    Waltz of the Waves.)

Y aún hay calvas marchitas a la luna
y llorosos cabellos en los libros.
Un polisón de nieve, blanqueando
las sombras, se suicida en los jardines.

¿Qué será de mi alma que hace tiempo
bate el récord continuo de la ausencia?
¿Qué de mi corazón que ya ni brinca,
picado ante el azar y el accidente?)

Exploradme los ojos, y, perdidos,
os herirán las ansias de los náufragos,
la balumba de nortes ya difuntos,
el solo bamboleo de los mares.

Cascos de chispa y pólvora, jinetes
sin alma y sin montura entre los trigos;
basílicas de escombros, levantadas
trombas de fuego, sangre, cal, ceniza.

Pero también, un sol en cada brazo,
el alba aviadora, pez de oro,
sobre la frente un número, una letra,
y en el pico una carta azul, sin sello.

Nuncio —la voz, eléctrica, y la cola—
del aceleramiento de los astros,
del confín del amor, del estampido
de la rosa mecánica del mundo.

The bald are still with us, turning doddering pates to the
    moon,
and the souvenirs soaked with their tears and preserved
    between covers.
The bustle found in the snow is the corpse in the garden
whose suicide brightens a shadow for good or for evil.

And what of my soul? How long has it been
since it broke all the records for absence and won
all the marathon prizes? What to do with a heart, between
    chance
and disaster—taunted by one or the other, yet numb in the
    middle?

Look me straight in the eyes: they focus on nothing;
they strike at you, shipwrecked; they stab you with derelict
    fears.
A blow of bad weather is massing its fronts to the north
and spending its force on the teetering void of an ocean.

Cartouches of sparks and gunpowder, bareback
equestrians with no heart for the fight in the wheat,
basilicas battered to rubble, gouts of ashes and blood,
pillars of quicklime and fire rising upward like waterspouts.

Still—there is dawn's aviatrix, holding a sun
in each arm, a goldfish in space,
with a numeral stamped on her forehead and a capital
    letter
and the bluest of envelopes caught in her beak, without
    postage.

Divinest of go-betweens—electrically wired in the rump
and the vocal cords—bearing news of the hurrying stars;
of Love's happy encirclement; and the exploding
machine of the rose that inhabits a universe.

Sabed de mí, que dije por teléfono
mi madrigal dinámico a los hombres:
¡Quién eres tú, de acero, rayo y plomo?
—Un relámpago más, la nueva vida.

(*Falta el último pliego*)

Guía estival del paraíso
(*Programa de festejos*)

Hotel de Dios: pulsado por los trenes
y buques. Parque al sur. Ventiladores.
Automóvil al mar y los andenes.

San Rafael, plumado, a la Cantina,
chofer de los colgantes corredores,
por un sorbete lleva, sin propina.

¡Al Bar de los Arcángeles! De lino,
las cofias de las frentes, y las alas,
de sidra y plumas de limón y vino.

Por una estrella de metal, las olas
satinan el marfil de las escalas
áureas de las veloces pianolas.

¡Campo de Aviación! Los serafines,
la Vía Láctea enarenada, vuelan
la gran Copa del Viento y los Confines.

Take it from me: my high-tension madrigal is burning
the wires. I am calling direct. I mean to get under your
    skins.
"You, there—whoever you are—lead, tinfoil, or sheet-
    metal: Are you there?"
"Another light in the thunderstone. The new life begins."

(Last Page Missing)

Summer Guidebook to Paradise
(*Festival Program*)

Hôtel-Dieu: "God's Hostel": connections by train
and by pleasure boat. Parks to the South. Transportation
direct to the beach and the boardwalks. Air conditioning.
    Clean.

Tours to the bistros. Saint Raphael in the galleries
guides in his flying regalia,
for the price of a sherbet. (No gratuities, please!)

To the Bar of the Archangels. Linen coifs
rising stiff on the hairlines, applejack
wings, feathers of lemon and wine.

Christmas-tree stars, with wave after wave
on the keys of the quick pianolas, gilding
the treads and the risers, glazing the ivories.

Over the Airport: the Milky Way's borders,
a cobweb in space, with seraphim circling the rim
of the Cup of the Winds—at your orders!

Y en el Estadio de la Luna, fieros,
gimnastas de las nieves, se revelan,
jabalinas y discos, los luceros.

¡Reina de las barajas! Por los lagos
de Venus, remadora, a los castillos
del Pím-Pám-Púm de los tres Reyes Magos.

Carreras de los vírgenes cometas
en cinta, alrededor de los anillos
saturnales, de alcol las bicicletas.

¡Funicular al Tiro de Bujías!
¡Submarino al Vergel de los Enanos,
y al Naranjal de Alberti, los tranvías!

Hotel de Dios: pulsado por los trenes
y buques. *Hall* al sur. Americanos
refrescos. Auto al mar y los andenes.

Madrigal al billete del tranvía

Adonde el viento, impávido, subleva
torres de luz contra la sangre mía,
      tú, billete, flor nueva,
cortada en los balcones del tranvía.

Huyes, directa, rectamente liso,
en tu pétalo un nombre y un encuentro
      latentes, a ese centro
cerrado por cortar del compromiso.

And there in the Stadium's Lunar Arena—like
gymnasts of ice, livid
javelins and discuses, the stars of the morning arising.

On Lake Venus, the Player-Card Queen
leans on her paddle and steers
for the castles of Bing-Bang, the rubber balls and the
    Mages.

A fairway for immaculate
comets, conceiving bicycles spinning in whiskey
with Saturnian rings at their backs.

Chair lifts direct to the targets, the pigeons
and candles; the Tunnel of Love to the Troll
Gardens; trams to the Groves of Alberti. (Have an
    orange!)

Hôtel-Dieu: "God's Hostel": connections by train
and by pleasure boat. *Hall*, to the south. American
soda-pop. Cars to the beach and the boardwalk again.

Madrigal on a Tram Ticket

Where the wind rears its towers of light,
outbraving all things and assaulting my blood,
    ticket that blooms on the platforms
again and is gathered like flowers on the trams—

Straight as the crow flies, headlong and explicit in air,
in your petal a name and a latent
    encounter, you fly toward the seals of that center
where a pledged cancellation awaits you.

Y no arde en ti la rosa, ni en ti priva
el finado clavel, sí la violeta
       contemporánea, viva,
del libro que viaja en la chaqueta.

Not the bonfire that burns in the rose, nor a forfeit
of faded carnations; yours is the sign
   of the violet, contemporaneous and living,
that colors the book in a jacket and goes where the traveler
   goes.

A Vanished Grove: 2

What shadowy dagger slashed at my life, cutting me off, half-aware, from the light and the marble formality of my poems as they existed up to that time, from the songs never far from the fountains of common experience, from my boats in the salt inlets: what flung me bodily into that well of despond, that pit of obscurity where all veered away in an anguish of being, seeking a habitable world, a path to the pure air of being?

Whole worlds, turned against me—
a selfhood asleep,
undefended, and manacled.

Smarting from the roots of my hair to the quick of my fingernails, insomniac, drowning in yellow bile, biting my pillow, harried with grief. How much, in the dark and the light of the world as I knew it, had been inching me toward that abyss, boiling up like a levin from the maw of the precipice! Impossible loves, betrayal and shock at the moment of total surrender and trust; ravening jealousy, hatching crimes in cold blood under cover of darkness; a sad overcast of suicide friends, like mute bell clappers, dinting my skull; unconfessed covet and hate struggling to make itself known, to burst in the open like a bomb in a minefield, implacably; empty pockets where even the hand went unwarmed; infinite bypaths leading nowhere under the wind and the rain and the drought; a family, silent or indifferent to the magnitude of my battle, watching the set

A VANISHED GROVE: 2

of my jaw or the cast of my character while I dropped like a sleepwalker in a corridor of the house or sank to a bench on the garden path; infantile terrors battering me with remorse, with hell-fears and doubt, dim echoes of Jesuit schooldays when I suffered and loved by the bays of Cádiz; discontent with all I had written, with my breakneck impatience, avidly hurling me on, stopping at nothing, pell-mell, with hardly a moment to draw a calm breath—all this and much more, things inexplicable, contradictory, labyrinthine.

How to take action: to speak or cry out, give shape to that tangle of self-doubt, rise to new effort in the chasm of utter disaster that engulfed me? Submerging myself ever more deeply, burying myself deeper and deeper in my shambles, mired in my own rubble, splintered and smashed in entrail and bone? It was then that my angels first showed themselves to my sight—not in their Christian, corporeal guise, as icons of paint and engraving, but as implacable spiritual forces, kneading themselves into the most turbulent and sinister states of my nature. And so I cast them forth on the world in a rabble, reincarnations of all that was desolate, anguished, inhuman—the good and the terrible together, biding their time, circling and inhabiting me.

I had lost a whole paradise, the sum of my later existence, it may be—all that was purest and primal in youth, joyous, unvexed. All at once I found myself destitute, stripped of old azures, facing physical collapse, maimed once again in my faculties, wrecked in my intimate being. Little by little I withdrew from all contacts: from friends, coffee-talk, the Residencia, the city I lived in. A "guest of the clouds," I fell to scribbling in the dark without thinking to turn on a light, all hours of the night, with unwonted automatism, febrile and tremulous, in spontaneous bursts, one poem covering the other in a script often impossible to decipher in broad daylight. The idiom I used was whetted and dangerous, like a rapier's point. Rhythms exploded in slivers and splinters, angels ascended in sparks, in pillars of smoke, spouts of embers and ashes, clouds of aerial dust. Yet the burden was never obscure; even the most confused and nebulous songs found a serpentine life and took shape like a snake in the flames. The outward reality of things hemmed me in, pressed on my spirit, battered my caves and abysses with ever-increasing force, casting me out in the streets—a lunatic lava, a comet portending disasters to come. A malcontent poet: acrimonious, touchy, incorrigible, so ran the rumors. I envied and hated the lot of all others: how few were unhappy, or without family subsidy, or careers promising tranquillity—college professors, university journeymen of the world, librarians, government officials, tourism employees? . . . And I? What had I? Not so much as a high school diploma; a house ferret at odds with my own kind, plodding toward all points of the compass, spinning like a leaf, spouting rainwater from the holes in my shoe leather. I longed to work at any trade other than writing . . . I insisted: let it be well-digging, drilling, the grossest, the barest, the most abject mode of employment. . . . A way out of that cavern of fiends, the endless insomnia, the nightmare, must be found.

SOBRE LOS ÁNGELES
CONCERNING ANGELS

(1929)

Paraíso perdido

A través de los siglos,
por la nada del mundo,
yo, sin sueño, buscándote.

Tras de mí, imperceptible,
sin rozarme los hombros,
mi ángel muerto, vigía.

¿Adónde el Paraíso,
sombra, tú que has estado?
Pregunta con silencio.

Ciudades sin respuesta,
ríos sin habla, cumbres
sin ecos, mares mudos.

Nadie lo sabe. Hombres
fijos, de pie, a la orilla
parada de las tumbas,

me ignoran. Aves tristes,
cantos petrificados,
en éxtasis el rumbo,

ciegas. No saben nada.
Sin sol, vientos antiguos,
inertes, en las leguas

por andar, levantándose
calcinados, cayéndose
de espaldas, poco dicen.

Diluídos, sin forma
la verdad que en sí ocultan,
huyen de mí los cielos.

Paradise Lost

Across centuries
and the void of a world,
sleepless, I seek you.

Behind me, invisibly,
never grazing my shoulders,
my dead angel stands guard.

Where is that Paradise,
shadow, lately your home?
Ask it in stillness.

Unanswering cities,
mute rivers, peaks
of no echo, inarticulate seas.

Nobody knows. Men
tranced and upright on the beaches
at the stilled grave's verge,

with no thought for my presence. Wan birds
in a petrified singing, blind,
on their rapturous way,

knowing nothing.
Sunless and stopped,
old winds make their circuit

of leagues, lift up the ash
of their passing and rain down
on our shoulders, having little to say.

All Heaven dissolves:
the truth that it bound in its being
turns shapeless and shuns me.

Ya en el fin de la Tierra,
sobre el último filo,
resbalando los ojos,

muerta en mí la esperanza,
ese pórtico verde
busco en las negras simas.

¡Oh boquete de sombras!
¡Hervidero del mundo!
¡Qué confusión de siglos!

¡Atrás! ¡Atrás! ¡Qué espanto
de tinieblas sin voces!
¿Qué perdida mi alma!

—Ángel muerto, despierta.
¿Dónde estás? Ilumina
con tu rayo el retorno.

Silencio. Más silencio.
Inmóviles los pulsos
del sinfín de la noche.

¡Paraíso perdido!
Perdido por buscarte,
yo, sin luz para siempre.

El ángel falso

Para que yo anduviera entre los nudos de las raíces
y las viviendas óseas de los gusanos.
Para que yo escuchara los crujidos descompuestos del
    mundo

Here at Earth's end,
at the ultimate margin,
my eyes fix on nothing.

I search in the death
of my hopes for a portico's
green in the blackened abysses.

O shadowy threshold!
Caldron and spate of a world!
What a riot of centuries!

Away! Away with them all! What unspeakable
panic of shadows!
What collapses of spirit!

—Dead angel, arise
where you are! Light the way
home with your blazon!

Silence; ever more silence,
as eternity's pulsebeat
fails in the night.

Ah, Paradise, lost!
Seeking you here I am lost in myself
and my night is forever.

False Angel

That I might pass through the knot of the tuber,
the worm's habitation of horn,
and hear out the crackle and rasp of a world

y mordiera la luz petrificada de los astros,
al oeste de mi sueño levantaste tu tienda, ángel falso.

   Los que unidos por una misma corriente de agua me veis,
los que atados por una traición y la caída de una estrella me escucháis,
acogeos a las voces abandonadas de las ruinas.
Oíd la lentitud de una piedra que se dobla hacia la muerte.

   No os soltéis de las manos.

   Hay arañas que agonizan sin nido
y yedras que al contacto de un hombro se incendian y llueven sangre.
La luna transparenta el esqueleto de los lagartos.
   Si os acordáis del cielo,
la cólera del frío se erguirá aguda en los cardos
o en el disimulo de las zanjas que estrangulan
el único descanso de las auroras: las aves.
Quienes piensen en los vivos verán moldes de arcilla
habitados por ángeles infieles, infatigables:
los ángeles sonámbulos que gradúan las órbitas de la fatiga.

   ¿Para qué seguir andando?
Las humedades son íntimas de los vidrios en punta
y después de un mal sueño la escarcha despierta clavos
o tijeras capaces de helar el luto de los cuervos.

   Todo ha terminado.
Puedes envanecerte en la cauda marchita de los cometas que se hunden
de que mataste a un muerto,
de que diste a una sombra la longitud desvelada del llanto,
de que asfixiaste el estertor de las capas atmosféricas.

and bite on the petrified starlight, false angel,
you have set up your booths for the bypasser west of my
    dream.

You who ride my identical tides,
urged by a star's fall, yoked to a common betrayal, who see
    me
and listen: withdraw to the desolate voice in the ruins.
Hear the patience of stone crossing over toward death.

Do not break from the keep of those hands!

The spider fails, far from his web,
the ivy leaf bursts into flame and rains blood at the touch
    of a shoulder.
Moonlight shines through the bones of the lizard.
For all we remember of heaven,
the cold's rage will stiffen the edge of the thorn
or work in a fraudulent furrow
to strangle the last consolation of morning: the birds.
Those who ponder the living will encounter the muddy
    devices
of false and implacable angels,
somnambulist angels who keep watch on the stations of
    sloth.

What has it profited you?
The dankness lies close to the glass and beads to a point,
a nightmare of frost awakens the spike
and the scissors to freeze in the scream of a crow.

It is finished.
You have labored for nothing in the stale of a comet's
    explosion,
and murdered the murdered,
and spoken grief's longitude in a deathwatch for shadows,
and pressed for the death rattle there in the capes of the
    air.

El ángel bueno

Un año, ya dormido,
alguien que no esperaba
se paró en mi ventana.

—¡Levántate! Y mis ojos
vieron plumas y espadas.

Atrás, montes y mares,
nubes, picos y alas,
los ocasos, las albas.

—¡Mírala ahí! Su sueño,
pendiente de la nada.

—¡Oh anhelo, fijo mármol,
fija luz, fijas aguas
movibles de mi alma!

Alguien dijo: ¡Levántate!
Y me encontré en tu estancia.

Los ángeles colegiales

Ninguno comprendíamos el secreto nocturno de las pizarras
ni por qué la esfera armilar se exaltaba tan sola cuando la mirábamos.
Sólo sabíamos que una circunferencia puede no ser redonda

The Good Angel

That year, as I slept,
a presence I never awaited
paused at my window.

"Waken and walk!" And straightway
the feathers and swords were disclosed to me.

Beyond us, the seas and the summits,
wing, beak, and cloud,
sunrises, sunsets.

"Follow her there! Her dream
overhanging the void!"

"O blest consummation! Marble
at rest in the block; the lights, the unrest
of the waters at rest in my soul!"

"Wake and walk forth!" said the presence.
And I woke where you were.

Grammar School Angels

None of us guessed the nocturnal enigma of blackboards
or knew why the globe of the galaxies trembled up when
    we looked at it long.
What were we sure of? Circumference at times is unround;

y que un eclipse de luna equivoca a las flores
y adelanta el reloj de los pájaros.

   Ninguno comprendíamos nada:
ni por qué nuestros dedos eran de tinta china
y la tarde cerraba compases para al alba abrir libros.
Sólo sabíamos que una recta, si quiere, puede ser curva o
      quebrada
   y que las estrellas errantes son niños que ignoran
      la aritmética.

El ángel de los números

   Vírgenes con escuadras
y compases, velando
las celestes pizarras.

   Y el ángel de los números,
pensativo, volando
del 1 al 2, del 2
al 3, del 3 al 4.

   Tizas frías y esponjas
rayaban y borraban
la luz de los espacios.

   Ni sol, luna, ni estrellas,
ni el repentino verde
del rayo y el relámpago,
ni el aire. Sólo nieblas.

   Vírgenes sin escuadras,
sin compases, llorando.

the time in the flower can be wrong
and the clock in the bird run ahead in a lunar eclipse.

We knew nothing:
what put the India ink in our fingertips,
why night shuts its compasses and opens its books to the
    dawn.
Our wisdom was this: right angles can curve or break off, as
    you wish,
and the stars, like a child knowing little arithmetic, wander
    on.

The Angel of Number

Virgins with T-squares
and compasses, tending
the heavenly blackboards.

Angels of number,
musing and flying
out of 1 into 2, out of 2
into 3, out of 3 into 4.

The chalks, the cold sponges
barring and blotting
the glare of the void.

Neither crescent nor star, sun
or the thunderclap's
green, or the air,
or the bolt in the air. Only mists.

Virgins empty of T-squares
and compasses, weeping.

Y en las muertas pizarras,
el ángel de los números,
sin vida, amortajado
sobre el 1 y el 2,
sobre el 3, sobre el 4 ...

Los ángeles mohosos

Hubo luz que trajo
por hueso una almendra amarga.

Voz que por sonido,
el fleco de la lluvia,
cortado por un hacha.

Alma que por cuerpo,
la funda de aire
de una doble espada.

Venas que por sangre,
yel de mirra y de retama.

Cuerpo que por alma,
el vacío, nada.

Los ángeles muertos

Buscad, buscadlos:
en el insomnio de las cañerías olvidadas,
en los cauces interrumpidos por el silencio de las basuras.

And there on the carrion slates,
the angel of number,
a corpse in the mummy-cloth,
aloft on the 1 and the 2,
on the 3 and the 4 . . .

Angels of Mildew

A light gone wry,
like the stone in an almond.

A voice, not sound's,
but the storm's fringe
shorn by the ax.

No bodily soul,
but a double rapier blade
in a scabbard of air.

Nor veins to let blood,
but wormwood of bracken and myrrh.

And the soul of that body:
vacancy, void.

The Dead Angels

Search for them; search for them there
in the drainpipe's forgotten insomnia,
gutters blocked by a silence of garbage.

No lejos de los charcos incapaces de guardar una nube,
unos ojos perdidos,
una sortija rota
o una estrella pisoteada.

    Porque yo los he visto:
en esos escombros momentáneos que aparecen en las neblinas.
Porque yo los he tocado:
en el desierto de un ladrillo difunto,
venido a la nada desde una torre o un carro.
Nunca más allá de las chimeneas que se derrumban
ni de esas hojas tenaces que se estampan en los zapatos.

    En todo esto.
Mas en esas astillas vagabundas que se consumen sin fuego,
en esas ausencias hundidas que sufren los muebles desvencijados,
no a mucha distancia de los nombres y signos que se enfrían en las paredes.

    Buscad, buscadlos:
debajo de la gota de cera que sepulta la palabra de un libro
o la firma de uno de esos rincones de cartas
que trae rodando el polvo.
Cerca del casco perdido de una botella,
de una suela extraviada en la nieve,
de una navaja de afeitar abandonada al borde de un precipicio.

El ángel mentiroso

Y, fuí derrotada
yo, sin violencia,
con miel y palabras.

Where the puddle goes blank to the clouds:
the eye's devastation,
a ring that is broken,
a star trodden under.

I have seen them before:
revelations of rubbish that flash from the mist.
And touched them myself:
dead clods come to nothing, a downfall
of tiles from the tower and the barrow.
Under the chimney's debris, the print
of the leaf on our boot soles, there is nothing.

Nothing to hope for.
Only vagabond parings that go out with no flame,
desolation that batters old furniture
near the names and the symbols that grow cold on the
    walls.

Search for them, search for them there:
under the wax that buries the word on the page,
the name in the angle of notepaper
in the dust-devil's swirl.
There, by the bottle ignored in the grass,
the shoe sole lost in the snow,
the rust of the razor blade left on the edge of the precipice.

Deceiving Angel

So it happened,
with no visible violence, with honey
and words, I was broken.

Y, sola, en provincias
de arena y de viento,
sin hombre, cautiva.

Y, sombra de alguien,
cien puertas de siglos
tapiaron mi sangre.

¡Ay luces! ¡Conmigo!

Que fuí derrotada
yo, sin violencia,
con miel y palabras.

El ángel avaro

   Gentes de las esquinas
de pueblos y naciones que no están en el mapa,
comentaban.

   Ese hombre está muerto
y no lo sabe.
Quiere asaltar la banca,
robar nubes, estrellas, cometas de oro,
comprar lo más difícil:
el cielo.
Y ese hombre está muerto.

   Temblores subterráneos le sacuden la frente.
Tumbos de tierra desprendida,
ecos desvariados,
sones confusos de piquetas y azadas,

In the wilderness wind
and the sand,
unpeopled, in chains, and alone.

A shadow cast
by a stranger, while a hundred doors
to the centuries slammed on my blood.

O radiance! be with me yet!—

who was broken
with no visible violence, with
honey and words.

Angel of Avarice

Those loungers on street corners
in kingdoms and clans still unguessed by the map makers,
were speaking their minds:

"He's dead
and don't know it.
Sure, he'd hold up a bank if he could,
burgle the clouds and the stars, steal the gold from a comet
to buy something really high-class:
a piece of the sky, nothing less!
But he's dead as they die."

Now earthquakes bear down on his head
and graveplots jar open.
Anomalous echoes,
indeterminate noises, a clatter of pickax and spade,

los oídos.
Los ojos,
luces de acetileno,
húmedas, áureas galerías.
El corazón,
explosiones de piedras, júbilos, dinamita.

    Sueña con las minas.

Canción del ángel sin suerte

    Tú eres lo que va.
agua que me lleva,
que me dejará.

    Buscadme en la ola.

    Lo que va y no vuelve:
viento que en la sombra
se apaga y se enciende.

    Buscadme en la nieve.

    Lo que nadie sabe:
tierra movediza
que no habla con nadie.

    Buscadme en el aire.

El ángel de carbón

    Feo, de hollín y fango.
¡No verte!

swarm in his ears.
His eyes
are acetylene gases,
wet gold-leaf that shines from a balcony.
His heart,
an explosion of flint, jubilation, and dynamite charges.

And he dreams about mines.

Song of the Unlucky Angel

It was you, then, coming this way—
on the breaker that carried me in
and cast me away.

Look for me in the wave.

You who go with no thought of return:
a wind in the alternate dark
that blows itself out and burns itself back in a spark.

Look for me in the snow.

That presence whom nothing can know
yet tears at the world in its dearth
and converses with nothing on earth.

Look for me in the air.

Angel of Coals

Foul, in the lampblack and slime,
You are not for our eyes!

Antes, de nieve, áureo,
en trineo por mi alma.
Cuajados pinos. Pendientes.

Y ahora por las cocheras,
de carbón, sucio.
¡Te lleven!

Por los desvanes de los sueños rotos.
Telarañas. Polillas. Polvo.
¡Te condenen!

Tiznados por tus manos,
mis muebles, mis paredes.

En todo,
tu estampado recuerdo
de tinta negra y barro.
¡Te quemen!

Amor, pulpo de sombra,
malo.

El ángel rabioso

Son puertas de sangre,
  milenios de odios,
lluvias de rencores, mares.

¿Qué te hice, dime
  para que los saltes?
¿Para que con tu agrio aliento
me incendies todos mis ángeles?

Once poised in the gilt and the snow,
in the sleigh of my soul.
A clabber of pinetrees. The hillslopes below.

Now in the areaway,
in the filth and the coal.
Away with it all!

With the splintering dream in the attic.
The cobwebs. The moth and the ash.
A plague on such trash!

Soiled by a touch of your hands,
my walls and my chairs and my tables.

All
that is scored by the print of your memory
in black inks and mire—
give it all to the fire!

And that octopus, love, in the shadow:
evil, so evil.

Angel Enraged

These are the doorways of blood,
the millenial spites of the past,
the tempests of spleen, and the seas.

What infamous thing have I done
to call down such a flood?
Tell me: why set a torch to my angels
and blow with so bitter a blast?

Hachas y relámpagos
de poco me valen.
Noches armadas, ni vientos leales.

Rompes y me asaltas.
Cautivo me traes
a tu luz, que no es la mía,
para tornearme.

A tu luz agria, tan agria,
que no muerde nadie.

El ángel desengañado

Quemando los fríos,
tu voz prendió en mí:
ven a mi país.

Te esperan ciudades,
sin vivos ni muertos,
para coronarte.

—Me duermo.
No me espera nadie.

El ángel ángel

Y el mar fue y le dió un nombre
y un apellido el viento

The ax and the lightning
are paltry, and will not avail:
nor the clashing of arms in the night
nor a scrupulous wind in the sail.

You slash and you batter me.
I am flung toward a light
which can never be mine: I am jailed
by your whirlwind and whirled out of sight.

Toward the light of your bitterness, wormwood of wrath,
no taster has touched with his tooth.

Angel Undeceived

Blazing out of the frost
I was seized by your voice:
"Come to my kingdom!

"My cities wait for you there—
neither living nor dead,
with a wreath for your head."

"No one dreams of my coming.
I sleep soundly," I said.

Angel's Angel

And the sea was, and gave him a name.
Surnamed by the air,

y las nubes un cuerpo
y un alma el fuego.

La tierra, nada.

Ese reino movible.
colgado de las águilas,
no la conoce.

Nunca escribió su sombra
la figura de un hombre.

El alma en pena

Esa alma en pena, sola,
esa alma en pena siempre perseguida
por un resplandor muerto.
Por un muerto.

Cerrojos, llaves, puertas
saltan a deshora
y cortinas heladas en la noche se alargan,
se estiran,
se incendian,
se prolongan.

Te conozco,
te recuerdo,
bujía inerte, lívido halo, nimbo difunto,
te conozco aunque ataques diluído en el viento.

Párpados desvelados
vienen a tierra.

his flesh was a gift of the clouds,
and his soul, of a flame.

Earth gave him nothing.

In that mutable kingdom
suspended by eagles,
he knows nothing earthly.

Nor can shadow disclose to his pen
the profile of a man.

Soul in Torment

That soul in its torment, alone,
that soul in perpetual hurt, pursued
by a dead incandescence.
By a death.

Latches and doorways and passkeys
spring open to startle us.
Curtains of frost grown immense in the night,
subtle as vapor,
catch, kindle,
and lengthen.

I know you:
I remember you,
lackluster candle, hoar halo, spent nimbus.
You, my assailant, however enfeebled in wind.

A vigil of eyelids
descends on our world.

Sísmicos latigazos tumban sueños,
terremotos derriban las estrellas.
Catástrofes celestes tiran al mundo escombros,
alas rotas, laúdes, cuerdas de arpas,
restos de ángeles.

No hay entrada en el cielo para nadie.

En pena, siempre en pena,
alma perseguida.
A contraluz siempre,
nunca alcanzada, sola,
alma sola.

Aves contra barcos,
hombres contra rosas,
las perdidas batallas en los trigos,
la explosión de la sangre en las olas.
Y el fuego.
El fuego muerto,
el resplandor sin vida,
siempre vigilante en la sombra.

Alma en pena:
el resplandor sin vida,
tu derrota.

The lash of the earthquake despoils what we dreamt
and temblors demolish the stars.
The whole havoc of heaven and the trash of this world,
a rubbish of feathers and viols, the psaltery's string
and a boneyard of angels.

No one shall enter: no thoroughfare into that heaven.

Tormented, tormented forever,
a spirit in torment.
Always in counter-light,
overmastered by none and alone,
most lonely of spirits.

The bird strives with the ship,
and the man, with the rose,
sorties and routs in the wheatfields,
an explosion of blood in the breakers.
And the fire.
The slaughter of fire,
a dead incandescence
always watchful in shadow.

A soul in its torment:
the dead incandescence
your undoing.

SERMONES Y MORADAS
SERMONS AND SOJOURNS
(1930)

Sermón de la sangre

Me llama, me grita, me advierte, me despeña y me alza, hace de mi cabeza un yunque en medio de las olas, un despiadado yunque contra quien deshacerse zumbando.

Hay que tomar el tren, le urge. No lo hay. Salió. Y ahora me dice que ella misma lo hizo volar al alba, desaparecer íntegro ante un amanecer de toros desangrándose a la boca de un túnel.

Sé que estoy en la edad de obedecerla, de ir detrás de su voz que atraviesa desde la hoja helada de los trigos hasta el pico del ave que nunca pudo tomar tierra y aguarda que los cielos se hagan cuarzo algún día para al fin detenerse un sólo instante.

La edad terrible de violentar con ella las puertas más cerradas, los años más hundidos por los que hay que descender a tientas, siempre con el temor de perder una mano o de quedar sujeto por un pie a la última rendija, esa que filtra un gas que deja ciego y hace oír la caída del agua en otro mundo, la edad terrible está presente, ha llegado con ella, y la sirvo: mientras me humilla, me levanta, me inunda, me desquicia, me seca, me abandona, me hace correr de nuevo, y yo no sé llamarla de otro modo:

Mi sangre.

Sermon on Blood

Whatever summons me, cries out to caution me, overturns me and heaves me aloft, batters my head in the foam like an anvil, a pitiless anvil smashing all in its humming vibrations.

Entrain: there's no time to lose. But the last train is gone. There is nothing. It's your heart's blood, they say, that sends things careening toward morning, swallows them whole in the dawn like a bull bleeding its life away at the mouth of a tunnel.

I know. I consent: it is time—time to strike through the voice that transfixes all things, from the ice on the wheat to the beak of the bird that renounces the earth and waits for a day when the sky will be quartz and all grind to a halt for a moment, at last.

A terrible urge to lash out at the heaviest bolts of the doors, with my blood, at the years' utter ruin, the despoilers who come down in the dark and quake for the loss of a hand, or a foot in the trap of the ultimate crevice whose fumes blind the onlooker and give back a sound like a falling of water from an alien world: the terrible urge is upon me, is here with my blood, makes a slave of me: while something that shames me and heaves me aloft, undermines me and drowns me, still drains me, abandons me and puts all to flight again for which I know no name but:

My blood.

A Vanished Grove: 3

The passion for bullfighting of José María de Cossío, a recent recruit to our Góngora conclaves, and my very good friend, was the occasion one evening of my meeting, in the lobby of the Palace Hotel, an altogether extraordinary figure destined, after his shocking death in the ring, to heroize one of the noblest elegies [1] ever to pour from the pen of a Spaniard: Ignacio Sánchez Mejías, then wholly committed to the art of the bullring. (I put it that way because, shortly thereafter, under the surveillance of García Lorca, he was to make his debut as a playwright, an impresario, and the founder of a company of Spanish dancers headed by his friend, Encarnación López, "La Argentinita.") Though Ignacio was then in his full physical maturity, the passing of time had brought him to that threshold when, in the taxing art of tauromaquia, the feet fumble and falter, with a consequent impairment of buoyancy, grace, and precision—precisely those qualities which a younger hand and a late friend then in his heyday, Cayetano Ordóñez, "Niño de la Palma," possessed in such abundance.

I think I may say I was the first of my generation to know Sánchez Mejías intimately and be chosen as his friend. Ignacio was not a grass-roots *torero*, like so many of his calling. The son of a distinguished physician of Seville, he had completed several years toward his college degree; but his Andalusian *afición* for the bulls had led him to take his

[1] Alberti has in mind, of course, not his own poem on this subject, but Federico García Lorca's *Llanto por Ignacio Sánchez Mejías* (1935).

A VANISHED GROVE: 3

turn with the cape with other youthful enthusiasts from the pastures and uplands, among them his future brother-in-law Joselito, who commanded one of the great rapiers of all time. I will not attempt an account of Ignacio's impassioned and violent career as a bullfighter, already fervently recorded by José María de Cossío in his monumental treatise on *The Bulls*. I will speak only of my relations with Ignacio from the time of our first meeting to the era of the Spanish Republic.

A great bullfighter, yes; but also a commanding intelligence and a powerful identity in his own right. What a rare sensibility for poetry—especially the poetry of our own generation! And how unstinting in his love and vitality, dispensing his friendship to all!

> *Auras of Andalusian Rome*
> *gilded his head*

García Lorca was to say in his *Lament* for the death of Ignacio. For Ignacio, in his physique, as in all other things, was no Andalusian gypsy, but cut in a different mold: classical, temperate, precise, and severe—the mold of Trajan's Seville. For all his contemplative cast, his penchant for witty diversion was constantly apparent: indeed, there were times when he laid on the horseplay with too heavy a hand, and descended to the puerile. I have seen him shying chick-peas in the street, at the feet of the girls, blowing them out of a tube that he rapidly snatched from his pocket and returned to its hiding place. On the other hand, mustering his full force, he could strike a brave blow in the Conquest of Góngora, with the rest of us, lavishing hours on end on the preciosities of the *Soledades* and committing to memory the most trying and labyrinthine of Don Luis' arabesques . . .

It should be perfectly apparent that our generation was

not a solemn one: not even the most urbane of our talents, like Salinas, Guillén, Cernuda, Aleixandre. . . . The times were quite otherwise: we had no taste for sanctimony. . . . But my friendship with Sánchez Mejías was verging on the dangerous. For some reason, the great *diestro* of the bullring was determined to turn me into a *peón* of his fighting *cuadrilla*. A practical joke? Perhaps. None the less, his pigheadedness caused me some worry. It was his thought that I should see the bulls at close range; he therefore wired me from Seville, insisting I join him in Badajoz, the plaza he had chosen for my debut, where, as he planned things, I would limit myself to a modest pass or two at the bull and then withdraw to the barrier in my glittering sequins to see how a bullfight is fought. Needless to say, I did not comply. The incident so piqued him, however, that he redoubled his efforts to gratify his vagary. Since he was ferocious in the pursuit of his whims, escape was out of the question.

It was one evening in June that his *idée fixe* of showing me off as a fighter in a legitimate ring came to a head in Pontevedra, with Cagancho, Márquez, and himself as matadors and the Portuguese Simão da Veiga acting as picador. José María de Cossío observed the outlandish proceedings from a seat on a lower *tendido*. The crowning absurdity was the spectacle of myself, alone among all the toreros in the conventional silver and gold of their calling, dazzling the onlookers in a costume of orange and black usually worn by Ignacio himself as a gesture of mourning in behalf of the tragic death of his brother-in-law, Joselito. . . . It needed only the first charge of the bull, bursting into the open and passing between my chest and the barrier, tremendous and blinding, to make all clear to me in a moment. I understood then the astronomical distance that divided a man sitting down to his sonnets, and another erect on his feet, his body open to the sun, in the presence of that limitless, blind bolt, that oceanic presence of a bull just unleashed from the pen . . .

Leaving the Plaza, Mejías, as it were, cut off my pigtail—by which I mean he informed me my career with the bulls was now at an end. It had lasted exactly three hours. It was then—on that very same evening—that Ignacio unexpectedly retired from the ring, in anticipation of which he had dedicated the last bull of all to Cossío: "This bull," he said, "the last I will kill in the ring, I dedicate to you!" Thereupon he abandoned one intrepid adventure for another in which the chest wounds, it may be, are sometimes more deadly. He exchanged the sand of the bullring for the boards of the stage; he transformed himself from a killer of brave bulls into an artist in the theater.[2]

[2] Like many toreros who have announced their retirement from the ring, Sánchez Mejías was tempted to return. It was on the occasion of a corrida in Santander, in the August of 1934, some seven years later, that he met his death in the ring.

VERTE Y NO VERTE
TO HAVE SEEN YOU AND SEE YOU NO MORE

(1935)

Elegía
A *Ignacio Sánchez Mejías*

EL TORO DE LA MUERTE

    Antes de ser o estar en el bramido
que la entraña vacuna conmociona,
por el aire que el cuerno desmorona
y el coletazo deja sin sentido;

    en el oscuro germen desceñido
que dentro de la vaca proporciona
los pulsos a la sangre que sazona
la fiereza del toro no nacido;

    antes de tu existir, antes de nada,
se enhebraron un duro pensamiento
las no floridas puntas de tu frente:

    Ser sombra armada contra luz armada,
escarmiento mortal contra escarmiento,
toro sin llanto contra el más valiente.

                             (*Por el mar negro un barco
                              va a Rumanía.
                              Por caminos sin agua
                              va tu agonía.
                              Verte y no verte.
                              Yo, lejos navegando,
                              tú, por la muerte.*)

    Las alas y las velas,
se han caído las alas,
se han cerrado las alas,
sólo alas y velas resbalando por la inmovilidad crecida de
    los ríos,
alas por la tristeza doblada de los bosques,

Elegy
For Ignacio Sánchez Mejías

THE BULL OF DEATH

Before being, or coming to be in the bellow
that breaks from a womb, or moves
in a wind's gust numbed by the whiplash
that rides on the flick of a tail or is crushed by a horn:

In the secret discharge of the seed
that tempers the pulse of the cow
to its blood-heat and blends to its need
the bull's wrath still to be born;

before nothingness was, or creation,
the unflowering staves of your forehead
packed into the threads that hard intimation:

To live armed with a shadow, and challenge an armor of
    light,
to threaten the threatener: a death for a death,
a bull beyond pity and tears, confronting the brave.

> (*A ship on the Black Sea*
> *tacks toward Rumania,*
> *but your agony chooses*
> *a waterless way.*
> *To have seen you and see you no more!*
> *I, voyaging outward and far,*
> *you, toward your slaughter.*)

Feathers and sails,
the winged are brought low,
the feathers are furled,
only feathers and sails slither by in a tumid stagnation of
    rivers,
wings folded by grief in the forests,

en las huellas de un toro solitario bramando en las marismas,
alas revoladoras por el frío con punta de estocada en las llanuras,
sólo velas y alas muriéndose esta tarde.

Mariposas de rojo y amarillo sentenciadas a muerte,
parándose de luto,
golondrinas heladas fijas en los alambres,
gaviotas cayéndose en las jarcias,
jarcias sonando y arrastrando velas,
alas y velas fallecidas precisamente hoy.

Fue entonces cuando un toro intentó herir a una paloma,
fue cuando corrió un toro que rozó el ala de un canario,
fue cuando se fue el toro y un cuervo entonces dio la vuelta por tres veces al ruedo,
fue cuando volvió el toro llevándolo invisible y sin grito en la frente.

¡A mí, toro!

(*Verónicas, faroles,*
velas y alas.
Yo en el mar, cuando el viento
los apagaba.
Yo, de viaje.
Tú, dándole a la muerte
tu último traje.)

EL TORO DE LA MUERTE

Negro toro, nostálgico de heridas,
corneándole al agua sus paisajes,
revisándole cartas y equipajes
a los trenes que van a las corridas.

the print of the bull in the bog, and his desolate bellow,
a trembling of wings in the cold, like a rapier's point on the
    plain,
and the dying away of feathers and sails in the dark.

The butterfly, yellow and red, the death-fated one
rigid with mourning,
doves pinned in a glaze on the telephone wires,
seagulls brought down from the riggings,
the clatter and strain of cordage and sails,
and the day of the failing of feathers and sails, begun.

It was then that a bull's spite was turned on a dove,
that a bull charged to gall a canary,
a bull veered away and a raven paraded the ring three times
    round;
and returned to his place with the mute bird hid in his
    horns.

Charge again and have done!

> *(Faroles, veronicas,*
> *feather, candle, and sail:*
> *I move on a sea as they fail*
> *in a breath.*
> *I, voyaging outward,*
> *you yielding the last of your capes,*
>   *your slippers and sashes,*
> *to death.)*

THE BULL OF DEATH

Black bull, nostalgic for wounds,
turning landscapes to water with a toss of your horns,
rifling all baggage and documents, stamping your seal
on the railways that lead to the bullrings.

¿Qué sueñas en tus cuernos, qué escondidas
ansias les arrebolan los viajes,
qué sistema de riegos y drenajes
ensayan en la mar tus embestidas?

Nostálgico de un hombre con espada,
de sangre femoral y de gangrena,
ni el mayoral ya puede detenerte.

Corre, toro, a la mar, embiste, nada,
y a un torero de espuma, sal y arena,
ya que intentas herir, dale la muerte.

> *(Mueve el aire en los barcos*
> *que hay en Sevilla,*
> *en lugar de banderas,*
> *dos banderillas.*
> *Llegando a Roma,*
> *vi de banderillas*
> *a las palomas.)*

¿Para qué os quiero, pies, para qué os quiero?
　Los pies pisan la muerte,
poco a poco los pies andan pisando ese camino
por donde viene acompañada o sola,
visible o invisible, lenta o veloz,
la muerte.

¿Para qué os quiero, pies, para qué os quiero?

Me va a coger la muerte en zapatillas,
no en zapatillas para el pie del baile,
no con tacón para esas tablas donde también
suele temblar la muerte con voz sorda de pozo,

What dreams in the span of your horns, what
furtive anxieties redden your journeys,
what maze for the drenching and draining of matter
turn the shock of your rage on the sea?

He with the rapier, who whets your nostalgias—
your dream of the gout in the thigh and gangrene—
not even the herdsman can bring you to heel.

Charge at the sea, bull, charge and strike home in your
 rage.
Ride down the killer of spindrift in the brine and the sand,
whom nothing can save, and deal him the death that you
 willed.

> *(Wind stirs in the ships*
> *of Seville;*
> *where a banner should fly,*
> *banderillas are poised for the kill.*
> *And arriving in Rome*
> *I see in the square of the doves*
> *the two banderillas.)*

How shall you serve me, feet, how shall you serve me,
who tread down a death?
Little by little you come treading the clay
where, alone or attended by many,
invisible, visible, swift or by tardy degrees,
death comes this way.

How shall you serve me, feet, how shall you serve me?

Death will catch me in slippers—
not pumps for the feet of a dancer,
hard heels that beat on the boards
and summon a death-tremor, the voice from the depths of
 a well,

voz de cueva o cisterna con un hombre no se sabe si
   ahogado,
voz con tierra de ortigas y guitarra.

   ¿Para qué os quiero, pies, para qué os quiero?

   Unos mueren de pie, ya con zapatos o alpargatas,
bien bajo el marco de una puerta o de una ventana,
también en medio de una calle con sol y hoyos abiertos,
otros...

   Me va a coger la muerte en zapatillas,
así, con medias rosas y zapatillas negras me va a matar la
   muerte.
¡Aire!

   ¿Para qué os quiero, pies, para qué os quiero?

               (Por pies con viento y alas,
           por pies salía
           de las tablas Ignacio
           Sánchez Mejías.
           ¡Quién lo pensara
           que por pies un torillo
           lo entablerara!)

EL TORO DE LA MUERTE

   Si ya contra las sombras movedizas
de los calcáreos troncos impasibles,

the voice from the cave and the cistern, of the drowned
> man that offers no answer,
the thistle that works in the clod, the guitar.

How shall you serve me, feet, how shall you serve me?

Some die upright in their sandals and shoe leather,
framed by a doorjamb or seen through a window;
others drop to the pavement, midway in the street, in
> the potholes and glare of the morning;
and others . . .

Death will catch me in slippers; somewhere
death will murder me just as I am, pink stockings, black
> slippers—
Give me air! *

How shall you serve me, feet, how shall you serve me?

> *(How often, in feathers and wind,*
> *erect on his feet, Ignacio*
> *Sánchez Mejías*
> *strode from the boards † with the rest!*
> *That a bull standing small on his feet*
> *could hammer him there on the barriers—*
> *who could have guessed?)*

THE BULL OF DEATH

If now, in that shadowy counterplay—the wary
projection of dimmed and ineffable contours honed

---

* *Aire* here rendered literally, is an "almost sacramental shout that bullfighters utter to ask for lighter, more graceful runs" through the cape.—L. M.
† The wooden barricade that surrounds the arena. "Sánchez Mejías was famous for his *pases de muleta* (cape passes) performed with his back to the barrier, or while sitting on the barrier footrail provided to help the bullfighter over the barrier in emergencies— a more dangerous stance than fighting in the middle of the arena."
—L. M.

cautos proyectos turbios indecibles
perfilas, pulimentas y agudizas;

   si entre el agua y la yerba escurridizas,
la pezuña y el cuerno indivisibles
cambian los imposibles en posibles,
haciendo el aire polvo y la luz trizas;

   si tanto oscuro crimen le desvela
su sangre fija a tu pupila sola,
insomne sobre el sueño del ganado;

   huye, toro tizón, humo y candela,
que ardiendo de los cuernos a la cola,
de la noche saldrás carbonizado.

   *(En la Habana la sombra
de las palmeras
me abrieron abanicos
y reboleras.
Una mulata,
dos pitones en punta
bajo la bata.*

   *La rumba mueve cuernos,
pases mortales,
ojos de vaca y ronda
de sementales.
Las habaneras,
sin saberlo, se mueven
por gaoneras.*

   *Con Rodolfo Gaona,
Sánchez Mejías
se adornaba la muerte
de alegorías:
México, España,
su sangre por los ruedos
y una guadaña.*

to a luster and pointed, seen against
branches and brackets of bone, impassively—

If, between water and precarious grass,
the cleft in the hoof, the indivisible horn,
should turn the impossible into the possible,
grinding the air into powder, slashing light into ribbons:

If crime such as this can awaken your blood
to its bafflement or harden your eyeballs to pore
on the dream of the slumbering herd, alone and unsleep-
    ing—

Flee from the smoke and the tinder, O firebrand bull
ablaze from your tail to the stock of your horns,
whom the darkness will blacken to cinder.

> *(In Habana, the shady*
> *palmetto*
> *rippled a fan for me, made*
> *revoleras.*
> *A mulatto,*
> *her nipples under her wrapper*
> *like horns tilted upward and ready.*
>
> *A rhumba moved in the horns*
> *in perilous passes,*
> *cow-eyes stood guard*
> *over seeding and growing.*
> *Unknowing, the girls of Habana*
> *turned like a cape, with the graces*
> *of Rodolfo Gaona.*
>
> *And Sánchez Mejías*
> *contended with death for the glories*
> *of Rodolfo Gaona*
> *and adorned it with allegories.*
> *Mexico, Spain*
> *both with his blood in their rings*
> *and a stain like a scythe.*

*Los indios mexicanos
en El Toreo,
de los ¡olés! se tiran
al tiroteo.
¡Vivan las balas,
los toros por las buenas
y por las malas!*

*Ya sus manos, Gaona,
paradas, frías,
te da desde la muerte
Sánchez Mejías.
Dále, Gaona,
tus manos, y en sus manos,
una corona.)*

¿Qué sucede, qué pasa, qué va a pasar,
qué está pasando, sucediendo, qué pasa,
qué pasó?

La muerte había sorbido agua turbia en los charcos que
    ya no son del mar,
pero que ellos se sienten junto al mar,
se había rozado y arañado contra los quicios negros de los
    túneles,
perforado los troncos de los árboles,
espantado el silencio de las larvas,
los ojos de las orugas,
intentado pasar exactamente por el centro a una hoja,
herir,
herir el aire del espacio de dos piernas corriendo.
La muerte mucho antes de nacer había pensado todo esto.

Me buscas como al río que te dejaba sorber sus paisajes,
como a la ola tonta que se acercaba a ti sin comprender
    quién eras
para que tú la cornearas.

*At El Toreo that day
the Mexican Indians
crowded the stands
and cheered themselves hoarse.
"Long live the bulls!
And long live the bullets,
for better or worse!"*

*Dying, he gives you
his handclasp still numbed
with the cold!
Give him, Gaona,
the gift of your hand
in his hands
and the crown for his head.)*

What moves, what is happening there, what is coming to pass,
what is happening, moving, passing,
or has come to an end?

Death drank from the stale of the puddles left by the tide that still feel the sea-salt,
death has grated and ground on the pylons that blacken the tunnels,
cankered the tree-trunks,
struck fear in the silence of larvae
and the eyes of the maggot,
death has planted itself in the pith of the leaves
with its passion to mangle,
to wither the spaces of runaway feet in the air.
Long before death was, it had worked some enormity there.

Oh, you harry me down like a river that gave you to drink
of its landscape, like an idiot ripple approaching, never guessing your guile,
to be tossed on your horns.

Me buscas como a un montón de arena donde escarbar un hoyo,
sabiendo que en el fondo no vas a encontrar agua,
no vas a encontrar agua,
nunca jamás tú vas a encontrar agua,
sino sangre,
no agua,
jamás,
nunca.

No hay reloj,
no hay ya tiempo,
no existe ya reloj que quiera darme tiempo a salir de la muerte.

*(Una barca perdida
con un torero,
y un reloj que detiene
su minutero.
Vivas y mueras,
rotos bajo el estribo
de las barreras.)*

EL TORO DE LA MUERTE

Al fin diste a tu duro pensamiento
forma mortal de lumbre derribada,
cancelando con sangre iluminada
la gloria de una luz en movimiento.

¡Qué ceguedad, qué desvanecimiento
de toro, despeñándose en la nada,
si no hubiera tu frente desarmada
visto antes de nacer su previo intento!

Mas clavaste por fin bajo el estribo,
con puntas de rencor tintas en ira,
tu oscuridad, hasta empalidecerte.

You hollow me out like a pillar of sand,
knowing nothing of water remains by the rift in the wall,
nothing of water wells up,
only blood
where the brine was,
nothing
of water
at all.

We die clockless
and timeless; and the dial
that might grant us its grace of escape now stands still in
    a timeless denial.

> *(A ship goes down*
> *where the bullfighter stands,*
> *and the clock holds the seconds*
> *at bay in its hands.*
> *Catcalls and ovations*
> *crash under the planks*
> *where the bullfighter braces a foot, and*
>   *are one.*

THE BULL OF DEATH

At length, to your brooding intention
you gave perishing form: a bull brought to his knees
in a splendor of pikes, in the pomp of the lights'
scintillations, undone by a dazzle of blood.

How paltry that blindness—all that animal
arrogance hurling its bulk into nothingness—
if in the close of your skull, unarmed and already foreseen,
the fated necessity had not been intended at all!

You lunged for the stirrups, you drove underneath
the maniacal red of your points, in your rancor,
till your swarthiness paled and your malice was sated.

Pero luego te vi, sombra en derribo,
llevarte como un toro de mentira,
tarde abajo, las mulas de la muerte.

> (*Noche de agosto arriba
> va un ganadero,
> sin riendas, sin estribos
> y sin sombrero.
> Decapitados,
> toros negros, canelas
> y colorados.*)

Se va a salir el río y ya no veré nunca el temblor de los
    juncos,
va a rebosar el río paralizando el choque de las cañas,
desplazando como una irresistible geografía de sangre que
    volverá los montes nuevas islas,
los bosques nuevas islas,
inalcanzables islas cercadas de flotantes tumbas de toros
    muertos,
de empinados cadáveres de toros,
rápidas colas rígidas que abrirán remolinos,
lentos y coagulados remolinos que no permitirán este
    descenso,
este definitivo descenso necesario que le exigen a uno
cuando ya el cuerpo no es capaz de oponerse a la atracción
    del fondo
y pesa menos que el agua.

Desvíeme esos toros,
mire que voy bajando favorecido irremediablemente por el
    viento,
tuérzale el cuello al rumbo de esa roja avalancha de toros
    que le
empujan,
déjeme toda el agua,
le pido que me deje para mí solo toda el agua,

Then, while the afternoon failed, I saw you again,
a shadow in ruins, a mountebank's fraud
of a bull, borne deathfully outward, by mules.

> (*In the August night*
> *the herdsman toils up*
> *without bridle or stirrup*
> *and no hat for his head;*
> *and a black bull*
> *roams headless*
> *with the roan and the red.*)

The river will flow out of sight and the reed shake no more,
the banks will brim over and the storm in the marshes go
    numb.
A bloody geography displaces all things: islands, where
    peaks rose implacably,
where the woods were,
unapproachable islands ringed by the watery graveyard of
    bulls.
There the bull's bulk heaves up,
the tail's lash goes taut and unleashes a whirlwind,
the laboring eye of the whirlwind that prepares for the pull
of all that compels us and would carry us under
as the body goes helpless and feels the attractive abyss
and is lighter than water itself.

Call off your bulls.
See: I go under, befriended by winds to the last.
Turn back and brace for that avalanche, the scarlet
    stampede of the bulls.
I want only water,
the total horizon of sea for my own:
the jet in the river,

agua libre,
río libre,
porque usted ya está viendo, amigo, cómo voy,
porque usted, viejo amigo, está ya comprendiendo adónde
    voy,
ya estás, amigo, estás olvidándote casi adónde voy,
amigo, estás, amigo ...

    Había olvidado ahora que le hablaba de usted, no de tú,
    desde siempre.

                        (*¿De dónde viene, diga,*
                        de dónde viene,
                        que ni el agua del río
                        ya le sostiene?
                        Voy navegando,
                        también muerto, a la isla
                        de San Fernando.)

DOS ARENAS

    Dos arenas con sangre, separadas,
con sangre tuya al son de dos arenas
me quemarán, me clavarán espadas.

    Desunidas, las dos vendrán a unirse,
corriendo en una sola por mis venas,
dentro de mí para sobrevivirse.

    La sangre de tu muerte y la otra, viva,
la que fuera de ti bebió este ruedo,
gloriosamente en unidad activa,

    moverán lunas, vientos, tierras, mares,
como estoques unidos contra el miedo:

the gout breaking free in the stone.
Friend, you who know how things stand with me now,
old friend, who have fathomed me out
and seem almost oblivious now,
friend who seem almost . . .

That my intimate word, grown so formal, cannot summon
    you now I had almost forgotten.

> *(Where do you come from*
> *speak out that land:*
> *all the weight of the river*
> *cannot buoy up that head.*
> *"Dead as I am,*
> *I tack like yourself with the dead*
> *toward the island of San Ferdinand.")*

TWO SANDS

Two sands and two blood-lettings: two
separate sands, with your blood in the sound of the sand:
they burn like a holocaust and break me on rapier points.

Yet the two will be single again, the broken
be joined in my veins and made whole
in my solitude and survive from within:

The blood of your death, and that other who, living,
moved out of your range to drink deep in the circling
    arena,
brilliant in singleness—these movers and shakers together,

these two will untether the shores and the oceans,
the moon and the weathers in one rapier-thrust against
    fear:

la sangre de tu muerte en Manzanares,
la sangre de tu vida
por la arena de México absorbida.

*(Verte y no verte.
Yo, lejos navegando,
tú, por la muerte.)*

Plaza de toros EL TOREO
*México
13 de agosto
1935*

Manzanares will speak for the blood of your dying,
while your life-blood runs out in a bullring of Mexico here
and is drained by the Mexican dust.

> (*To have seen you and see you no more!
> I, voyaging outward and far,
> you, on the flood of your dying.*)

Plaza de toros EL TOREO
Mexico
13 August
1935

A Vanished Grove: 4

On March 6, 1939, I left Spain,[1] my doomed and adorable country, for Oran. [Shortly after], rebellion broke out in the Fortress of Cartagena, where the monarchical colors were raised on the barricades. Hours later, in Madrid, Colonel Seigismundo Casado struck his blow against the Negrín regime, making a gift of our tough and invincible capital, intrepid and exquisite Madrid—for two years the wonder of the world—to Generalissimo Franco. En route to Oran we went off-course and almost crashed into Melilla.[1] Minutes after our landing in Oran, another plane rolled down the runways of the airport, carrying La Pasionaria.[2] The whole heart of Spain had been betrayed and sold out once again.

Oppressed in the whole of my being by the spilling of the noblest blood of my country, explosions still rocking my ears, I walked the streets of Paris, having found temporary asylum with the great-spirited Pablo Neruda, then Chile's angel of mercy to all Spaniards in exile, on the banks of the Seine, 31 Quai de l'Horloge. In the August of that year, in the struggle to survive, and avoid, at all costs,

---

[1] Alberti here alludes to the final phase of the Spanish Civil War, in which, as the poems in *Capital de la gloria* will indicate, he was actively engaged in the heroic defense of his capital. Melilla, also mentioned (then Spanish Morocco), had been a Franco stronghold since 1936.

[2] Dolores Ibarruri, member of the Executive Committee of the Communist Party and symbol of militant dedication to the Loyalist cause; a Basque whose evangelical fervor endeared her to the rank and file as "La Pasionaria."

A VANISHED GROVE: 4

the enforced charity of a fear-ridden, inglorious France, María Teresa and I accepted, at the urgent insistence of Picasso, a modest offer from Radio Paris-Mondial, to serve as translators—routine translators—for their broadcasts beamed to Latin America. What was the outcome of those months—what can I show for them now? Little or nothing. I saw only the starvation, persecution, and death of very good Spaniards, the day-by-day exile of many old friends fleeing the mainland of Europe forever. . . .

[Soon enough] the youthful director of Paris-Mondial, M. Fraisse, favored me with a confidential and plaintive announcement: no one less than Marshal Pétain himself, recently queued on the doorstep of Generalissimo Francisco Franco, like an ordinary sergeant, had solemnly bound the government of *La France Eternelle* to our instant dismissal from radio broadcasting, in view of the clear and present need of propitiating the "One Spain" of the caudillo. . . .

"*Votre travail comme* speaker, *mes chers amis, était excellent . . . mais . . . c'est le Maréchal. . . . Vous comprenez. . . ?*"

"*Oui, M. Fraisse,*" we answered him gratefully, "*nous sommes fiers d'être mis à la porte de la France de votre noble Maréchal . . .*"

Je quitte l'Europe . . . like Rimbaud; but not to trade horses or scour the burning deserts. I abandoned Europe, my very own Europe, to confront all the more squarely the lot of the displaced Spaniard, the expatriate pilgrim of hope, seeking a path to the soil of America. . . . At the port of Oran, under a broad roof of darkness, I saw the volunteers of another Foreign Legion of exiles form and pass in review: the pure gold of Spain, now debased, almost all of them students, professors, laborers, farmers, heroes of that most stupendous of all conflicts, chosing a

A VANISHED GROVE: 4

hard and hazardous life to the alternative of dying piecemeal in French concentration camps—death in the conquest of despair, even flight . . .

I wept from the marrow of my bones, to see them: ill-clad and somber, dwindling away in a column, delivering themselves up to the blazing bosom of Africa, fated never to leave it again . . .

Still tortured with sleeplessness, just before daybreak, I took my last look through the porthole of my cabin: Gibraltar. The Rock: the black tail of the poor bull of Spain, now usurped, menacing, lying wounded in the mist and the blood of the water. And there, under the silvery arcs of the dolphins and the beaches beyond Tarifa, there returned for a moment a feckless vision of orchards that bordered on schoolyards, the gold of the dunes, and the wraith of myself, on the seashore, unfettered . . . Casablanca. . . . The Canaries, unattainable, forbidding. . . . Dakar. . . . [America, Buenos Aires, Argentina]. . . . A long journey, an exodus fearful and long, in which, for the first time in my life, I felt the whole mainland of Europe swoon away in my blood.

CAPITAL DE LA GLORIA
CAPITAL OF GLORY
━━━━━━━━━━━━━━
(1938)

Los soldados se duermen

Contémplalos.

                  Dormidos, con un aire de aldea,
de animales tiernísimos, duros y acostumbrados
a que de pronto el sueño les coja donde sea,
como a los incansables perros de los ganados.

   Sobre una pesadumbre parecida a un paisaje
batido por pezuñas y osamentas rendidas,
mordiéndoles el lento son de un mismo rodaje,
solas y ausentes ruedan las pupilas dormidas.

   Duermen, sí, con las manos, que son puños, abiertas,
un instante olvidadas del reciente ejercicio
de dejar las contrarias vidas turbias desiertas.
... Mas también los fusiles descansan de su oficio.

Los campesinos

   Se ven marchando duros, color de la corteza
que la agresión del hacha repele y no se inmuta.
Como los pedernales, sombría la cabeza,
pero lumbre en su sueño de cáscara de fruta.

   Huelen los capotones a corderos mojados,
que forra un mal sabor a sacos de patatas,

Soldiers Asleep

Consider:

       For they sleep with a countryman's air,
with the vulnerable look of the animal—these stark ones, inured
to the slumber that fells them, however they fling themselves forward,
tirelessly, sooner or later, like shepherd dogs there.

Over their sufferance, as over a land's depredation
stricken with hoofprints, a country of withering bone,
the bite of a wheel and the slackening sound of rotation
spins from their pupils asleep, estranged and alone.

They sleep: and their hands that are fist-blows, unhuddle,
an instant unlearning their calling, the names and the numbers,
the bodies abandoned behind them, like the murk in a puddle,
. . . And even the rifle gives over its office, and slumbers.

Country Recruits

They march flintily forward, the color of bark
slashed by the ax's aggression, immutable.
Like splinters of adamant, the heads and the faces are dark,
but a glow flashes out of their dream like the husk of a fruit.

An odor of clothing goes up: lamb's wool rank with the rain—
a reek as of burlap and gathered potatoes that moves

uncido a los estiércoles y fangales pegados
en las cansinas botas más rígidas que patas.

Sonando a oscura tropa de mulos insistentes,
que rebasan las calles e impiden las aceras,
van los hombres del campo como inmensas simientes
a sembrarse en los hondos surcos de las trincheras.

Muchos no saben nada. Mas con la certidumbre
del que corre al asalto de una estrella ofrecida,
de sol a sol trabajan en la nueva costumbre
de matar a la muerte, para ganar la vida.

Monte de El Pardo

Tanto sol en la guerra, de pronto, tanta lumbre
desparramada a carros por valles y colinas;
tan rabioso silencio, tan fiera mansedumbre
bajando como un crimen del cielo a las encinas;

este desentenderse de la muerte que intenta,
de acuerdo con el campo, tanta luz deslumbrada;
la nieve que a lo lejos en éxtasis se ausenta,
las horas que pasando no les preocupa nada;

over mud and manure and clings to whatever remains
in the mash of their boot soles and hardens the leather like
    hooves.

Their sound in the darkness is obdurate: mule teams and
    burros
fanning out in the streets and blocking the doors and the
    gutters,
they pour from the fields like a mountain of wheat in the
    kernel
and plant themselves deep in the trenches like seeds in a
    furrow.

They know nothing, have little to say. Their conviction is
    this:
to advance with all possible speed on the threatened
    assault of their star,
to labor from sunrise to sunrise in another employment
dealing death to their deaths and winning their lives in a
    war.

On the Slopes of El Pardo

Suddenly, sun over slaughter: such a stunning return
of that brilliance to squander on valleys and mountains!
Such maniacal stillness and such savage tranquillity
moving down from the clouds, like a crime, over acorn and
    oak!
This ruse to annihilate dying, to conspire
with the whole of a landscape and burn in a sunburst of
    light,
so that even the snow seems remote in the unction of
    distance
and the hours in their passing know nothing at all of the
    fight—

todo esto me remuerde, me socava, me quita
ligereza a los ojos, me los nubla y me pone
la conciencia cargada de llanto y dinamita.
La soledad retumba y el sol se descompone.

A "Niebla," mi perro

"Niebla," tú no comprendes: lo cantan tus orejas,
el tabaco inocente, tonto, de tu mirada,
los largos resplandores que por el monte dejas
al saltar, rayo tierno de brizna despeinada.

Mira esos perros turbios, huérfanos, reservados,
que de improviso surgen de las rotas neblinas,
arrastrar en sus tímidos pasos desorientados
todo el terror reciente de su casa en ruinas.

A pesar de esos coches fugaces, sin cortejo,
que transportan la muerte en un cajón desnudo;
de ese niño que observa lo mismo que un festejo
la batalla en el aire, que asesinarle pudo;

a pesar del mejor compañero perdido,
de mi más que tristísima familia que no entiende
lo que yo más quisiera que hubiera comprendido,
y a pesar del amigo que deserta y nos vende;

How they sting my compunction, undermine what I am,
rob the grace from my vision, while the darkness increases
to batter my conscience with the dynamite charge of my
 grieving:
till stillness is strident again and the sun goes to pieces.

To "Misty," My Dog

Misty, you could never conceive it: though your ears ring
 with the truth
of it—all that innocent tobacco of your gaze, now a little
 demented;
all the pathless magnificence left on the slope of the
 mountain
where you bound like the supplest of rays that uncoils on a
 breeze.

Those castaway mongrels, now grown wary, or mad: look
at them well: they bolt from a rent in the fog, placing paw
after paw, with the timid estrangement of dogs, to pluck
out the heart of a mystery: a house that was theirs, in the
 rubble.

Despite all that panic cortege, the unceremonious
queuing of cars that carry their death in a box
in the barest of woods; or a child looking up at a lark
of a fight in the clouds that might batter him down as he
 looks—

For all the friends fallen, the pick of a lifetime now lost,
or that last desolation of all: a family cold
to all I would have them weigh well and conceive at all
 costs;
or the turncoats recoiled from our love, and sold out—

"Niebla," mi camarada,
aunque tú no lo sabes, nos queda todavía,
en medio de esta heroica pena bombardeada,
la fe, que es alegría, alegría, alegría.

nevertheless, Misty, dog at my heels, nevertheless,
for all you can never conceive, without knowing why,
at the heart of heroical anguish and endless bombardment,
ours is the faith in a world that is joy! that is joy! that is
    joy!

ENTRE EL CLAVEL Y LA ESPADA
BETWEEN SWORD
AND CARNATION
―――――――
(1941)

De ayer para hoy

Después de este desorden impuesto, de esta prisa,
de esta urgente gramática necesaria en que vivo,
vuelva a mí toda virgen la palabra precisa,
virgen el verbo exacto con el justo adjetivo.

Que cuando califique de verde al monte, al prado,
repitiéndole al cielo su azul como a la mar,
mi corazón se sienta recién inaugurado
y mi lengua el inédito asombro de crear.

Sonetos corporales: 3

Huele a sangre mezclada con espliego,
venida entre un olor de resplandores.
A sangre huelen las quemadas flores
y a súbito ciprés de sangre el fuego.

Del aire baja un repentino riego
de astro y sangre resueltos en olores,
y un tornado de aromas y colores
al mundo deja por la sangre ciego.

Fría y enferma y sin dormir y aullando,
desatada la fiebre va saltando,
como un temblor, por las terrazas solas.

From Yesterday for Today

After this willful derangement, this harassed
and necessitous grammar by whose haste I must live,
let the virginal word come back to me whole and meticulous,
and the virginal verb, justly placed with its rigorous adjective.

While it qualifies meadow and mountain to speak of their green,
or invokes all the sky, repeating its blue to the ocean:
let the whole heart be moved to its depths, as though all had not been,
and the tongue in my mouth touch the awe of unwritten creation.

Corporeal Sonnets: 3

That smell in the air: blood mingled with lavender,
moving up in the dazzle of fragrances: a scent
as of blood and scorched flowers, an odor
of fire like a hemorrhage of cypress and fir.

Suddenly out of the air, a downpour
of planets and blood dissolved in their odors:
a tornado of hues and aromas that bloodies
and blinds what it touches and effaces a universe.

Sleepless and ailing, baying aloud to the cold,
a fever unleashes its blazing degrees, a tremor
works in the earth and climbs toward the desolate terraces.

Coagulada la luna en la cornisa,
mira la adolescente sin camisa
poblársele las ingles de amapolas.

Sonetos Corporales: 7

Nace en las ingles un calor callado,
como un rumor de espuma silencioso.
Su dura mimbre el tulipán precioso
dobla sin agua, vivo y agotado.

Crece en la sangre un desasosegado,
urgente pensamiento belicoso.
La exhausta flor perdida en su reposo
rompe su sueño en la raíz mojado.

Salta la tierra y de su entraña pierde
savia, venero y alameda verde.
Palpita, cruje, azota, empuja, estalla.

La vida hiende vida en plena vida.
Y aunque la muerte gane la partida,
todo es un campo alegre de batalla.

And see! where a crescent of moonlight has clotted the
 cornices:
a girl who moves nakedly there, the nude adolescent
sowing herself in the poppies and sending them out of her
 loins.

Corporeal Sonnets: 7

The stilled heat grows in the groin; in the silence
of surf, a flicker of spray turning over.
The tulip's magnificence that thrives in a hardness of
 wicker,
bends back in its drought and continues, alive and ex-
 hausted.

A power lives on in the blood: a kindling vagary,
uneasy, insistent, belligerent, granting no quarter.
All that was lost to the flower or forgotten in lethargy
breaks out of sleep and forces its roots toward the water.

The very cobbles leap up: out of the clay of its entrails,
resins unload, wellsprings, the green of the poplars.
All trembles and crackles, strains forward, lashes out, and
explodes.

Life cleaves to life, splits asunder to magnify life.
And however death forces its forfeits or gains its advan-
 tage,
the fields lie before us for battle, and the battle is jubilant.

De los álamos y los sauces

(*En recuerdo de Antonio Machado*)

10

Anda serio ese hombre,
anda por dentro.
Entra callado.
Sale.

Si remueve las hojas con la tierra,
si equivoca los troncos de los árboles,
si no responde ni al calor ni al frío
y se le ve pararse
como olvidado de que está en la vida,
dejadle.

Está en la vida de sus muertos, lejos,
y los oye en el aire.

From Poplar and Willow

(Homage to Antonio Machado) *

10

A man with a taciturn air,
who walked from within:
who came, having little to say,
and went as he came.

If he stripped the boughs bare as the clay
and was lost in the tree trunks,
if he felt neither burning nor chill,
if we saw him bemused in his tracks,
denying his lifetime, stock-still, with the way back
forgotten; do not trouble him there.

He lives deep in the life of the dead and the dying,
and hears in a faraway air.

* "1939: Now that a great part of our army are either in French concentration camps or awaiting betrayal in Madrid, I have heard over radio in the freezing January night, of the death in Colliure of our Antonio Machado. All is over."—R. A., "Autobiographical Index"

14

A ti, enterrado en otra tierra.

Perdidos, ¡ay, perdidos!
los niños de la luz por las rotas ciudades
donde las albas lentas tienen sabor a muerto
y los perros sin amo ladran a las ruinas;
cuando los ateridos
hombres locos maldicen en las oscuridades,
se vuelcan los caballos sobre el vientre desierto
y solamente fulgen guadañas repentinas;

entonces, que es ahora,
pienso en ti, en esa noble osamenta abonando
trigos merecedores de más verdes alturas,
árboles que susurren tu nombre dignamente,
y otro cielo, otra aurora
por los que te encontraras tranquilo, descansando,
viéndote en largo sueño remontar las llanuras,
hacia un clamor de torres erguidas al poniente.

Pienso en ti, grave, umbrío,
el más hondo rumor que resonara a cumbre,
condolido de encinas, llorado de pinares,
hermano para aldeas, padres para pastores;
pienso en ti, triste río,
pidiéndote una mínima flor de tu mansedumbre,
ser barca de tus pobres orillas familiares
y un poco de esa leña que hurtan tus cazadores.

Descansa, desterrado
corazón, en la tierra dura que involuntaria
recibió el riego humilde de tu mejor semilla.

14

To you, buried in foreign soil.
Fallen! O fallen!
the children of light in the broken cities
where gradual dawns taste of death
and the yelping dogs run wild in a desolation;
where the madman stiffens with cold and curses in darkness, where
hunger topples the horse on an empty belly
and only the headlong flash of the sickle surprises us;

then, which is always and now,
I remember a splendor of bones
in the wheat, that should kindle a greener plateau,
trees honoring you with a sigh,
and other skies, other sunrises
for those who can guess at your peace or touch your serenity,
seeing you toil toward those plains from the depths of your dream
in a clamor of towers, upright, on a rim of the west.

I remember you, somber and shadowy one—
all that lies deepest in utterance rebounds from the peaks,
the grief of the evergreens, the tears of the pine groves,
blood brother and villager, father of goatherds;
I remember you, saddest of rivers,
and ask for a flowery tithe of your reticence,
your bare beach familiarly under my keel,
and a handful of firewood cut down by your thieving despoilers.

Sleep sound, expatriate
heart, in the flint that reluctantly
drinks your invincible seed like the humblest of dews.

Sobre difuntos bosques va el campo venidero.
Descansa en paz, soldado.
Siempre tendrá tu sueño la gloria necesaria:
álamos españoles hay fuera de Castilla,
Guadalquivir de cánticos y lágrimas del Duero.

En El Totoral
(*Córdoba de América*), 1940

Del pensamiento en mi jardín

El llorar tiene huesos,
amor, como las frutas.
Lágrimas de piñones.
Por eso al pensamiento cuando canta
se le hace un nudo en la garganta,
de ciruelas o melocotones.

Escúchalo, alhelí,
para contarlo luego al heliotropo:
pálida era mi madre, y carmesí,
cuando me la enterraron bajo un chopo.

Doblégate a la grama, trepadora,
pensamiento sin bridas.
¡Frena!
¡Freno!
Es toda oídos la azucena
y el amaranto moreno.

The fields of hereafter arise on the perishing forests.
Peace to you, soldier asleep.
The exigent glory is yours for a dreaming eternity:
the poplars of Spain arise, howsoever far from Castile,
the Guadalquiver of the canticles and the tears of the Duero.

In *El Totoral*
(Córdoba de América), [June] 1940

FROM *Thoughts in a Garden*

Grief has its bones, love,
like the stone in a fruit.
It can weep like the gums of the conifer:
when thought turns to song,
the knot that it draws in the throat
tastes of peaches and plums.

This was known to the clove
and disclosed to the heliotrope:
my mother was pale while she lived, but was rose
when they buried her under a poplar.

Unwind in the grasses, untrammeled
climber of pastures, grow long as a thought!
Strike as with bridle
and bit!
The whole of the lily lifts up, like an ear,
and the amaranth darkles.

PLEAMAR
FLOODTIDE
―――――
(1944)

*T*irteo

1

Tú eras cojo. Tirteo. Así estos cantos,
a los que faltan pies, pero no el alma.

2

¿Qué tienes, dime, Musa de mis cuarenta años?
—Nostalgias de la guerra, de la mar y el colegio.

3

¿En dónde está ese vientre, triste cueva,
ese varón, aquel instante oscuro?

4

En el día de la ira,
las bocas de las madres bajarán a los vientres.

5

Habrá matriz gozosa que conciba
una bala, un puñal premeditados.

6

Yo te defenderé.
                      —¿De qué manera,
si tú mismo te arrancas,
cada vez que eso dices,
pálido osado, un diente?

Tyrtaeus[*]

1

That limp of yours, Tyrtaeus, full of heart,
like my songs, though short an occasional foot!

2

What's left us, Muse of my Forties?
Nostalgias: the soldier's, the schoolboy's, the sea's.

3

Where is that cavern of sadness, the womb,
the virile young man, and the shadowy moment?

4

On the day of their wrath,
the mouths of the Mothers will descend to their wombs.

5

The womb will grow light and conceive
of a bullet, a bayonet poised for the kill.

6

"I'll stand by and defend you!"
                              —How so,
wan desperado, if, when all's said and done,
affirming these things, each time
you wrench out a tooth from your gums?

---

[*] Tyrtaeus, a Greek elegiac poet living in Sparta in the seventh century B.C., during the Messenian wars, and said to be a favorite of the Athenian army. Legend identifies him as a lame schoolmaster, and fragments of his marching songs are still extant. The ironical perspectives afforded to Alberti, as "poet in the street," are apparent.

7

Una bala y dos metros de tierra solamente
—les dijeron.
                Y el campo
dió en vez de trigo cruces.

8

El soldado en la nieve pensó que era palmera
y que se le llenaban de dátiles los brazos.

9

Y aquel alférez del desierto iba
sonámbulo entre sombras congeladas de pinos.

10

Hay muertos cuya paz merecería
ser quebrantada todas las auroras.

11

Yace el soldado. Vino
a preguntar por él un arroyuelo.

12

Pensé que al toque de diana iban
regresando los hombres a su alma.

13

¿Y por qué si yo oculto en el pecho una espada
no he de ocultarla dentro del pecho de los otros?

7

A bullet and two meters of earth: it suffices,
they told them.
              —And the field where the wheat was
reaped a harvest of crosses.

8

The infantryman in the snow dreamed he was changed to
   a palm:
that the fronds filled with fruit and he gathered the dates
   in his arms.

9

While the second lieutenant, asleep on his feet in the line,
slogged through the desert in the shadowy resin and pine.

10

Some have died whose repose should be blown
into bits, each day with the breaking of dawn.

11

Here lies a soldier. A trickle of water came
down to ask for some news of the front, in his name.

12

I thought when the bugles had blown and the reveille
sounded, we might still call the souls in our bodies our
   own.

13

Hiding a sword in my breast—why not daggers
to hide, at my need, in the breasts of the others?

14

En tus manos el mirto era tan verde
que nunca creció fuego
que hablara más lozano.

15

¡Oh, tapadme los ojos! ¡Aún más!
                              Y seguí viendo
a través del espanto helado de las manos.

16

¿Será posible un odio en carne viva
los años y los años?

Cuando se nos va alguien

Entonces,
se presentan, pasado ya ese último
estirón de la vida en que los trajes
se acortan, inservibles para el trago
de la entrega total al de la muerte;
se presentan quién sabe qué jardines,
qué rincones de alcobas, qué vestigios
de palabras amantes, qué apariencia
de agua dulce cruelmente arremansada.

Como por transparencia
se ve subir, abrir súbitamente,
más que jazmín, doblado jazminero,

14

The myrtle so green in his hands—
not even the voice in the furious pillar of fire
was more luxurious.'

15

Still more, then? I'll shut my eyes to it all!
                                             And
I looked at the chill of my fear through the space in my
    hand.

16

That flesh and blood loathing: still
with me, year in and year out—is it possible!

When Someone Is Lost to Us

Then
they show themselves to our eyes when the ultimate
shudder that shrivels their lives and their
clothing is over, and nothing avails
but to drink down the draught of the total surrender of
    dying;
there arises, from Heaven knows where, what remembrance
    of gardens,
a corner of bedroom, a litter
of tenderness spoken in love, a sense
of the sweetness of water that grows bitter and hardens.

As though caught behind crystal,
something climbs, something suddenly opens
more total than jasmine, or jasmine redoubled,

pura, desvanecida, delicada,
una tranquilidad de niña fuente,
de niña, aunque ligero
saltándole la voz, antepasada.

Era un jacarandá que, marinero,
se hizo a la mar. Su azul recién mojado
contra su azul, ya en tierra y jardinero,
subió, cantó, gritó más azulado.

Abuela.
Tú moriste en enero.
Estrella. Estela
de aquella más que barca, golondrina.

. . . Se presentan quién sabe qué rincones,
quién sabe ya qué ruinas de ruina
sentada ansiosamente, susurrando
penumbras de un humilde acabamiento,
mientras a las monteras entornadas
sube un llanto perdido de bodegas
entre un ahogarse oscuro de caballos.

Me llorarán los robles,
cuyas ardientes fibras, perfumadas
de las matrimoniales
soleras, hacen desvenar los pinos;
los pelargonios y amarilis dobles
que fermentan la flor de los añales,
pálidos, secos, enramados vinos.

Manteles.
Se acordarán de mí largos cristales,

a thing made exquisite, diminished, and pure:
the repose of the fountains of childhood,
of the girl in the fountain, her voice rising upward
    untroubled
to sing of the past as before.

The jacaranda weighed anchor and put out to sea
like a sailor. That drench of immediate blue,
wet blues over blue, gone underground with the gardener,
rises upward again, and sings, and is bluer for crying.

Grandmother.
You died on a January.
Starlike; or a bird
in the wake of the ship that is shallop and swallow
    together.

Corners rise up out of Heaven knows where,
the ruin of ruins for which no one can answer,
a planted anxiety and a shadowy
whisper of humbled finalities,
as the wail of despair forces its way from the vault
to a half-opened skylight
like a blind strangulation of horses.

The oak is my mourner
in its blazing contexture: the fragrance
that marries the beam to the crossbeam
and distills all the gums in the pine.
Let the twinned amaryllis and the spreading geranium
boil up from the flowers of the graveside bouquet
bled of color and parched, and leaven the boughs like a
    wine.

Tablecloths on a table.
The great goblets remember me,

satisfechos toneles,
lentos o repentinos
de sangre, más que azúcar, moscateles.

. . . Se presentan quién sabe qué retazos,
qué escombros de coloquios imprecisos
entre las acerolas desprendidas
o por el nisperal que el miedo instaba
a alzarse en un verdor de verderones.

Hermana.
¿Estás allí, di, estás por los balcones
del báncigo, escondida en la cochera,
ángela del pretil de la solana,
brisa transida por zarpar ligera?

. . . Mas de pronto, quién sabe qué agua dulce
cruelmente arremansada, qué cortinas
de yerto amor, qué ledos, familiares
designios, guardadores en su centro
de esas lisas almendras que al partirles
el corazón dan una leche amarga.

. . . Se presentan y no sé qué decirles.

Te has ido.
Te has muerto tú, y tu traje
final se te acortó violentamente.
Déjame aquí con lo que me has traído:
un resto de paisaje
y tu cuerpo presente.

the abrupt or the gradual
running of wines in the cask
and the blood that surpasses all sugars, the muscatel
   cramming the barrels.

. . . Pieces and clutter arise—Heaven knows what they
   mean—
such a nondescript rubbish of hawthorn, such a chatter
of loosening berries,
a quaking of leaves in the crab apple, and the fears
of the finch, sending volleys of green over green.

Sister.
Are you there? Do you move on the balconies, say,
or are you hidden away in the coach house,
a battlement angel invoking the sun and the water,
a languishing gust working faintly to fill out a sail?

. . . O ever more suddenly, how the sweet water
thickens and stales—Heaven knows how—and the stiff-
   ening
curtains close over love, while the whimsical, easy
inventions, the guardians there at the center, fail like the
blandest of almonds whose husk breaks apart
to pour out the milk of their bitterness over the heart.

. . . They show themselves now to our eyes, who have
   nothing to tell them.

You are gone.
You are dead, and what is left
of your clothing has ruthlessly withered you up.
Leave me now with the little you bring me:
the bones of a scene, and the scrap
of your body laid out like a gift.

A Vanished Grove: 5

Few have been as convinced as I was at fifteen that their true vocation lay in the arts of painting and drawing. . . . In the Casón [1] of King Philip IV, under the most ravishing allegory suspended by Giordano from the ceilings of the main hallway, I reverentially copied in all sizes the white plaster casts holding all the airy luminosity of the Victory of Samothrace, the vaulting outlines of the Discobolus of Myron, the tapered simplicities of the Apoxyomenus of Lyssipus, the infinite torment of Laocöon, the shaggy musculature of Hercules, the infantile bouyancy of the Faun with the Goat. . . . In a few months I knew the Casón by heart. . . . Without abandoning my sketches entirely, I went on to explore other media whose difficulty I guessed at a glance: I set up my easel in the Prado and worked as a copyist. For the first of my efforts I chose a dead Saint Francis, attributed to Zurbarán.

I have not yet spoken of the wonder I felt on the occasion of my first visits to that treasure of a picture gallery. Nursed on the mediocrity of tinted reproductions and some landscapes in the "school of Velázquez" that found their way to our little Andalusian village and the walls of my grandfathers, I had thought—heaven knows why—that all the painting of the past was by nature murky, sallow as a clod, alien to all the azures, the reds and the pinks, the golds, the green and the white that suddenly burst like a revelation in the paintings of Velázquez, Ti-

---

[1] The Museo de Reproducciones in Madrid.

A VANISHED GROVE: 5

tian, Tintoretto, Rubens, Zurbarán, Goya . . . Disclosed to that innocent gaze—not without an initial, indefinable blush—were the opalescent splendors of the flesh tints of Rubens, the power of the Graces, overflowing Pomonas, nymphs fleeing through forests, Dianas adorned with trumpets and dogs, tall Venuses with girdles unbound, nude goddesses, flooding the nocturnal watches of an adolescent and filling him with unrest. Till then, I had known little of satyrs or fauns, centaurs, tritons and all the rest of that bucolic and watery company, all with that flush in their pupils, muscles tensed in the consummation of gods, caught by the brush of a Rubens in the roses and jasmine . . . In the whole school of Venice, in Titian, in the Maytime of Veronese' murals, in the hot golds of Tintoretto, I recognized, without puzzling it through, how much azure and white, how much sun and Mediterranean air had been packed into the marrow of my Italo-Andalusian bones. These, day by day, raced in a ripened fulfillment of naked refinement, the golden age of color, the unutterable image of erotic desire, of passion unfettered and crammed with the whole of the senses. I had thought, calling to mind the few reproductions in books and magazines I had seen at my Aunt Lola's, that not only the gloom of the colors, but the subject of classical painting itself was religious, and that nothing but devils and angels, virgins, Christs, saints, popes, monks and nuns of all orders filled the walls of museums. How shockingly the immense central gallery of the Prado was to alter that provincial illusion! . . . For I came to understand that, notwithstanding the aerial grays, the silvers and azures and pinks of Velázquez, the heavenly nebulosities of Murillo, the incandescent blues of El Greco, the ivories and whites of Zurbarán, the chromatic intensities of Goya, my blood and my vision belonged wholly to that world of green and gold pagandom, of which Titian—and Tie-

A VANISHED GROVE: 5

polo!—above all others was absolute master. It was he, more than all other painters, his exact feeling for radiance in art, who confirmed in me, beyond all possible doubt, that my roots went down to those civilizations of azures and whites—all I had soaked up since childhood in the common facades of El Puerto, in the doorframes and windows of the villages there by the bay, darkened a little by those bluer transparencies which come to us from the frescoes of Crete, traversing all Italy, blueing the whole Mediterranean littoral of Spain, from the hamlets of Cádiz and the Atlantic, as far up as Huelva and the boundaries of Portugal.

A LA PINTURA
HOMAGE TO PAINTING
(1948)

A la paleta

A ti, infinita haz, campo sembrado
donde siega el pincel, gavilla, amasa
y entre color, luces y sombras, pasa
de mar radiante a tiempo anubarrado.

A ti, pozo y brocal, donde asomado
medita, viene y va, mide, acompasa;
frente asida a la mano que traspasa
tu ojo de Polifemo enamorado.

A ti, abanico, ala redonda, escudo,
espejo que al vestir queda desnudo
y nuevamente superficie pura.

En ti se cuece la visión que nace.
Tu firmamento el arcoiris pace.
A ti, lecho y crisol de la Pintura.

Negro

1

Y abrió un hoyo en lo claro, un agujero
desde el que dijo:
                —Soy también hermoso.

A Palette

I invoke you, infinite sheaf of the sown field
where the brush gleans its harvest, cluster
that gathers its grasses together in the dark and the light of
    the colors,
and moves from the sea's scintillations to a cloudier
    weather.

Yours is the sill of the well where, bemused by the water,
we come and we go in our wonder, we divide and
    apportion:
Polyphemus' one eye, transfixed like the gaze of a lover
by a hand moving always beyond it, like a beast on its
    tether.

You are fan, and the arc of a wing; you are shield,
and the glass of a mirror that mirrors you naked,
however you lay on your colors, yielding pure surface
    again.

You are caldron and dream's fermentation that quickens,
sky where the span of the rainbow can graze, like a
    meadow,
hearthstone where Painting flames out, and the bed where
    it lies.

Black

1

Black opened a well in the brilliance
and spoke from the pit:
                    "I too am comely."

2

Tuve forma de vaso, negro ánfora,
cielo para los dioses del Olimpo.

3

Negro como la tinta, negro como
la que linea el cuerpo del dibujo,
la que muerde la sombra del grabado.

4

Negro de España, negro
de los cinco sentidos:
negro ver,
negro oír,
negro oler,
negro gustar y negro
—¡oh Pintura!— tocar!

5

Soy un negro mortaja sepultado.
Mi entretejida eternidad yacente
finará mucho antes
que la amarilla y dura de los huesos.

6

El negro olor a cirios apagados.

7

Negro misa solemne Zurbarán.

8

Tu eres la luz con antifaz. Lo quitas.
Pero sus ojos siguen siendo negro.

2

The metamorphoses of the urn: in the amphora's blackness
a sky for Olympian gods.

3

Ink blacks: the bounding
black line that embodies our images
and bites in the dark with the burin.

4

Spanish black: the five senses
blackened:
black sight
and black sound,
black smell
and black taste; and the painter's black,
black to the touch.

5

Black of the burial cloths:
the sleep of my woven eternity
will not outlive
the yellowing horn of the bones.

6

The black smell of ritual candles—blown out.

7

High Mass in the blackness of Zurbarán.

8

The personae of light. Unmask.
Still the blackness looks out of your eyes.

9

Soy el hermano del papel, reluzco
en él como caminos paralelos.

10

Tuve siempre un temblor, una caricia
vaporosa en la mano de Manet.

11

Cuando soy puro, cuando
soy tan total como una pared blanca,
respondo por Juan Gris, Braque, o Picasso . . .

Azul

1

Llegó el azul. Y se pintó su tiempo.

2

¿Cuántos azules dió el Mediterráneo?

3

Venus, madre del mar de los azules.

4

El azul de los griegos
descansa, como un dios, sobre columnas.

5

Pinceles que son plumas,
azul añil, cuando de ti se tiñen.

9

I blaze out of pulp, with a
parallel path for my papery brother.

10

There was always that tremor, that airy
caress in the hand of Manet.

11

Most purely of all,
intact and entire like the white of a wall,
I answer Juan Gris and Picasso and Braque.

Blue

1

Blue was; and then painted itself into Time.

2

How many blues make a Mediterranean?

3

Venus, the inlander's mother-of-blues.

4

The blue of the Greeks:
columnar, asleep upon plinths like a god.

5

Wings seize our brushes
when we dip them in indigo.

6

Venecia del azul Tiziano en oro.

7

Me enveneno de azules Tintoretto.

8

Azul azufre alcohol fósforo Greco.
Greco azul ponzoñoso cardenillo.

9

Explosiones de azul en las alegorías.

10

En el azul Manet cantan los ecos
de un azul español en lejanía.

11

El mar invade a veces la paleta
del pintor y le pone
un cielo azul que sólo da en secreto.

12

Tiene el azul estático nostalgía
de haber sido azul puro en movimiento.

13

Aunque el azul no esté dentro del cuadro,
como un fanal lo envuelve.

6

The Venice of Titian: a blueness gone gold.

7

I poison myself with the blue Tintoretto.

8

The phosphors and alcohol blues of El Greco.
The venom-and-verdigris blues.

9

In azure explosions: the allegories.

10

The blues of Manet: Spanish blue, sung
like a faraway echo.

11

Sometimes the sea overflows
on the palette, and surrenders its secret
in sky-color, washes of heaven.

12

Blue remembers some marvel of motion—
when having been blue was immaculate.

13

Canvas cannot contain it: but
blue circles the square like the bell of the lamp.

Rojo

1

Lucho en el verde de la fruta y venzo.

2

Pleno rubor redondo en la manzana.

3

Rojo para el descanso de los hombros
y la espalda de Venus
—Giorgione—dormida.

4

Me levanto hasta el solio de la púrpura
y desciendo esparcido—¡oh Greco!—en pliegues.

5

El púrpura a través de los cristales
—copa, vaso, botella—
calientes de los vinos.

6

Un rosa con escarcha, de Velázquez.

7

Bajé hasta el rosa rosa de Picasso.

8

Como el clavel que estalla en los ceñidos
marfiles de unos senos apretados.

Red

1

I strike through the greens of the fruit, and prevail.

2

The apple's full flush in the round.

3

Red in the shoulder's repose
and the haunches of Venus:
the drowsing Giorgione.

4

I climb the king's purples
and descend with El Greco in the scattering
    draperies.

5

Purples caught through cut glass—
goblet, decanter, and cup—
in the warmth of the wine.

6

The rose in the frost of Velázquez.

7

I descend to the rose of the rose of Picasso.

8

Carnation explosions, erect
in the ivory round of the tightening nipple.

9

Como el grana fugaz de una amapola.

10

Pensad que ando perdido en la más mínima,
humilde violeta.

11

Soy el infierno—Brueghel,
Bosch—y el nocturno espanto
en los ojos insomnes de los niños.

Blanco

1

Mi vieja historia es la pared. Si buscas
deslumbrarte conmigo,
recréate los ojos en su tirante frente.

2

Blanco de Creta, tibio,
caliente, casi azul, reverberante.

3

Yo vi—Rafael Alberti—
la luz entre los blancos populares.

4

Mi infancia fué un rectángulo
de cal fresca, de viva
cal con mi alegre solitaria sombra.

9

The poppy in fugitive cochineal.

10

Think how I dwindle away
in the least of the violets.

11

Brueghel's and Bosch's inferno:
the night-hag that stares
from the eyes of insomniac children.

White

1

Walls are my history. To recover
that wonder, feast your eyes
on the thrust of those surfaces.

2

The whiteness of Crete: ablaze or lukewarm,
almost blue in its backward reflections.

3

I—Rafael Alberti—have seen it:
light lives in the popular whites.

4

My childhood: a whitewashed
rectangle, wet quicklime
and the joy of my shadow that prints it alone.

5

Yo soy el hijo de la cal más pura.

6

Soy el más albañil de los colores.

7

Una línea, una letra,
sobre mí. ¡Inolvidable maravilla!

8

Una línea, una letra,
un rayón solamente en blanco tiza
sobre el terso nocturno de los pizarras.

9

De pronto caigo como traje o nube.

10

Soy a veces el arco ágil de un potro
contra el azul sin límites.

11

Aquel—Uccello—viejo pajarillo,
muerto en la araña de la perspectiva,
me hizo saltar en forma de caballo.

12

Soy mantel, alba, níveo
encaje en el cristal de las heladas.

5

Call me quicklime's immaculate son.

6

I: master builder of colors.

7

One line or one letter
above me: indelible marvel!

8

One line or one letter,
one chalk stroke
compact in the blackboard's mute nocturne.

9

I fall swiftly like a cloud or a drapery.

10

At times, the mercurial curve of a colt
seen against limitless blue.

11

Uccello, that old one, that bird
dead in the nets of perspective,
made me hurdle the hedge like a thoroughbred.

12

I am altarcloth, alb, and the needlepoint
freeze in the snow-crystal.

13

Aparezco en el sueño como hálito,
como sombra marfil
de plato—Zurbarán—, mantel o monje.

14

Blanco puro, total, mas prisionero
en un cuadrado, un círculo, un triángulo.

15

Recordad que también yo soy la rosa.

Al pincel

   A ti, vara de música rectora,
concertante del mar que te abre el lino,
silencioso, empapado peregrino
de la noche, el crepúsculo y la aurora.

   A ti, caricia que el color colora,
fino estilete en el operar fino,
escoba barredera del camino
que te ensancha, te oprime y te aminora.

   A ti, espiga en invierno y en verano,
cabeceante al soplo de la mano,
brasa de sombra o yerta quemadura.

   La obstinación en ti se resplandece.
Tu vida es tallo que sin tierra crece.
A ti, esbelto albañil de la Pintura.

13

I take shape like a breath in a dream
in the ivory shadows of Zurbarán:
on a platter, a cloth, or a monk.

14

Pure white—the whole of the white—is most jailed
by the circle, the square, and the triangle.

15

Never forget: white is also the rose.

A *Paintbrush*

Baton that conducts us to music, sea's
virtuoso that tacks toward an ocean of canvas—to you,
pilgrim of silence and wayfarer drenched in a voyage
whose time is the midnight's, the dusk's, and the dawn's.

Caress that the colors have colored,
stylus that tempers its point for a master's employment,
broom to sweep clean and open the way to a journey,
enlarging, confining, diminishing itself for your pleasure.

You are wheat in the tassel, that ripens for summer and
    winter,
tossed and returned by the gust that moves under my
    hands,
live coal for a furnace of shadow, or banked conflagration.

Whatsoever resists or opposes, grows resplendent in you,
who live like the stalk of a flower and thrive beyond earth
and stand comely and tall on the stem, master builder of
    Painting.

Velázquez

Se apareció la vida una mañana
y le suplicó;
             —Píntame, retrátame
como soy realmente o como tú
quisieras realmente que yo fuese.
Mírame, aquí, modelo sometido,
sobre un punto, esperando que me fijes.
Soy un espejo en busca de otro espejo.

*

Mediodía sereno,
descansado
de la Pintura. Pleno
presente Mediodía, sin pasado.

*

. . . Y entraba por la puerta de tus cuadros
al encinar, al monte, al cielo, al río,
con ecos de ladridos, de disparos
y fugitivas ciervas diluídas
en el pintado azul de Guadarrama.

*

Conocía los troncos y las hojas,
la herradura en la tierra,
la huella del lebrel
y hasta esas briznas
que en las sombras no son más que el alivio
del pincel que al pasar las acaricia.

*

La majestad del cielo
sobre la melancólica

from "Velázquez"

One day, Life appeared to Velázquez,
saying:
      "Paint me. Paint me
as I am in reality, as your painter's reality
supposed I might be.
I will wait for you there, your submissive
exemplar poised on a point, till you fix me forever,
a mirror in search of a mirror."

*

Midday
serenely at rest
in the Picture. Midday eternally
present, without future or past.

*

. . . And opened a door in the Painting
into oak groves and mountains, the sky and the river,
hounds and the echoing gunfire and
the fugitive stag: the azure and oils
of the blue Guadarrama dissolved in your colors.

*

And knew them: the leaves and the tree trunks,
the hachure of hooves in the turf,
 the track of the greyhound,
and even that stir in the air
whose shadowy byplay remembers
the peace of the brush that stroked what it touched, and
    moved on.

*

Heaven's whole majesty:
and below, a grand melancholia

majestad de la encina que guarece
la tristeza cansada de un retrato.

*

La pintura en tu mano se serena
y el color y la línea se revisten
de hermosura, de aire y "luz no usada".

*

Yo me entré —soy el aire— en el cuadrado
abierto de las telas, en los regios
salones, en las cámaras umbrías,
y allí envolví los muebles, las figuras,
revistiéndolo todo, rodeándolo de ese vívido hálito que hoy
hace decir:
            —Mojaba su tranquilo
pincel en una atmósfera oreada.

*

Dice el pincel:
            —Como también soy río,
lo envuelvo todo a veces
en un vaho de plata.

*

La tenue rosa y gris argentería.

*

Dice el borracho:
            —Tengo
noble cara de príncipe y borracho,
de príncipe borracho o de beodo
que fuera rey y borracho a un mismo tiempo.

of oak that encircles
the nostalgic depletion of Painting.

*

The Painting grows calm,
in your hands. Color and line
are clothed in fair raiment: "unaccustomed," inviolate
    light
and the air.

*

"I entered the hazardous web of the canvas,"
said the air, "in the throne rooms
of power and the shade of the bedchamber,
to encompass what waits for me there:
a nimbus on people and furniture, a garment
ringing all in one vivid halation."
                              "He drenched
the repose of his brush in ethereal space," said the watcher.

*

Said the brush:
            "I was always
part river. I encompass all being, at my pleasure,
in subliminal silver."

*

The tentative rose and the livid brocades.

*

Said the drunkard:
                "Mine
is the nobler demeanor of princes and tosspots:
the king in his cups, or the prince
who is tosspot and tyrant at once."

*

¿Quién el más noble príncipe? ¿El que alza
el arma cazadora entre sus guantes
o el perro que a sus pies mira tranquilo?

*

Sangre azul en los perros de Velázquez.

*

Y un lebrel:
             —Sí, llamadme
S. M. Felipe Lebrel IV.

*

Mas también los caballos le podrían
disputar a los perros la corona.

*

Hago sonar los niños como rubias
campanas repicadas de colores.

*

Los negros como túmulos,
los trajes negros como monumentos.

*

La distinción le dijo ante la lámina
rigurosa y exacta de un espejo:
—Tengo un nombre. Me llamo...
Y el pintor retrató su propia imagen.

*

Which is nobler? The prince touching his glove
to the steel of his fowling piece, or that other—
the dog looking tranquilly up, at his heel?

*

Blue blood for the hounds of Velázquez.

*

Said the greyhound:
                "You may call me
His Highness King Philip the Greyhound the Fourth."

*

The horses may also contend with the dogs
for the royal succession.

*

I make children sing out like blond
bell-metal, a volley of carillon color.

*

The blacks, like a catafalque:
Monumental blacks in the folds of the clothing.

*

Perfection looked from the finical
panes of the mirror and said to him:
"There are names for images. You may call me . . ."
But the painter had painted another: his own.

Miguel Ángel

(*Fragmentos*)

1

No las Gracias, las Furias, las frenéticas,
desesperadas Furias
te acunaron de niño. Fueron ellas
el Ángel de la Guarda de tu sueño.

2

Clamó por ti el Señor,
te llamó por tu nombre allá en las cimas
en donde extraviado, antiguo y loco,
habla consigo mismo,
mordiéndose en voz baja su secreto.
—Miguel Ángel—te dijo—. Y en tu mano,
cerrándola, lo puso.
                Y tú la abriste.

3

Mirad aquí al violento,
al desnudo, al hambriento
de Eternidad.
Para él la Belleza
es la santa, la fuerte,
poderosa Tristeza
con quien a vida o muerte
lucha la Humanidad.

4

Mirad aquí al amado del rayo y la tormenta,
al pobre solitario de las olas,
al perdido del mar y de las playas.

from "Michelangelo"

(*Fragments*)

1

Not cradled by Graces, but Furies:
the demoniac ward
of the desperate ones, the angel
guarding the child and the dream of the child.

2

Called by your name by your God
and brought to a mountainous place
where the Lord of the mysteries, grown addled and old
and insane, communes with Himself
and harrows the depths with His voice:
"*Michelangelo!*"—A secret was placed in your hands, and
your fingers closed over.
      And you opened the fist of that hand.

3

To this violent man,
naked and starved
for Eternity,
Beauty came in the guise
of the Sadness that lives in all powerful things—the wrath
of our grieving Humanity
that encounters the holy and strenuous,
and contends for a life, for a death.

4

Call him beloved of the storm and the thunderbolt,
recluse of waves, and
the flotsam tossed up in the brine and the sand.

Ved al arrebatado torbellino que se levanta a nube,
el ala del espíritu temible,
la tromba que se expande en los espacios,
los cubre, los inunda y los golpea
para descender humo incandescente,
lava de luz, ceniza alumbradora.

5

Pincel en soledad, pincel hundido
en lo oscuro, llenando
de ráfagas de luz y de temblores
de tierra todo el cielo.
Sólo por ti la cara desvelada de Dios,
pincel movido al soplo de trompetas finales,
pudo ser descubierta entre las nubes.

6

Por las calles de Roma, nieve y viento,
desolado nocturno, levantándole
fuego a las piedras, ráfaga de sombra,
alguien galopa, eco de trueno antiguo,
casi extinguido ya, solo, ¿hacia adónde?

No es grande la campiña, no es inmensa
la mar aún para guardar el último
relámpago salvado de su sueño.
Tal vez la mar, oh Dios, pero montaña,
no de espumas y olas, sí de cumbres
congeladas, de mármol, sí de simas
de pétreos sordos ríos torrenciales.
Tal vez allí, tal vez allí . . .
                              Y galopa.

But see how the maw of the whirlwind ascends to the
    cloud,
the wings of ineffable spirit,
the verge of the waterspout widening out into space
to envelop all distance and batter the void, like a flood,
and return to us here in a nimbus of smoke, light's lava,
the holocaust left in the cinder.

5

The brush in its solitude, undone
by the darkness; the brush
in a temblor of light, charging the earth and the air
with the might of its cross-currents:
yours was that loneliest vision—the manifest face of your
    God
in the cloud, the path of the brush to the blast
where the horns of apocalypse rouse us at last.

6

Wind and ice in the streets: Roman snow
and the desolate night of the rider who gallops
alone, kicking fire from the cobble—
whose flight is an echo of thunder, subsiding,
a gust of old chaos, and who spurs—toward what haven?

The terrain is not infinite; the sea
that might salvage the last incandescence of things,
a scintilla he dreamed of, is not boundless.
Might it be toward a sea? A mineral sea like an alp—
God help us!—a sea not of spindrift and waves, but of
pinnacles hardened to marble, petrified summits,
stopped watersheds, spates of detritus and stone.
And then, might it be . . .
                        And he gallops.

Lleva en su mano el rayo, la postrera
exhalación, la chispa final. Todo
pudiera ser de nuevo iluminado:
la Creación, recién nacida al día,
el palpitante verbo nunca oído.
No son las bridas, no, las que en sus dedos
se estrujan. Es la última centella.
Lo saben sólo un viejo y un caballo.
Va a abrir la mano, va a soltarla. ¿Adónde?
Tal vez al mar, al mar, pero de roca.
¡Peñas del mar, montes del mar, canteras!
Allí tal vez . . .
     Y las espuelas sangran.

Bloques ya guerreados, sometidos,
cinceladas entrañas, escondidas
médulas de la piedra, atrás, pasando,
ya estatuas olvidadas de la noche,
entre la compasión de las ruinas.
Atrás, los puentes vistos sólo en sueño,
la ciudad de su honor fortificada,
los natales jardines agredidos,
dioses de su niñez entre las hojas:
allí el fauno riendo, el torso roto,
brotado nueva fuente de la tierra.
Pero ya todo es súbito delirio
por ver la cara de la luz y hablarle.
Y oye su galopar como un solemne
son de martillos de una antigua cólera.

Atrás, rompiendo, aplastadora, inmune,
salta la arquitectura, blanco cíclope
furioso, en el azul tendiendo arcos,

His hands hold our last scintillations,
death rattles, thunderbolts. All
that might blaze with the life of another awakening,
the day of the parting of waters, the unspeakable
word that might shake all Creation.
He strives, not with bridle and bit, but the ultimate
thunderstone clasped in his fingers—
an old man and a horse and a secret between them.
He shall presently open that hand and unleash it—on
    what?
On a sea, it may be, on those breakers of flint, it may be:
on that torrent of adamant, canyons of ocean, sea-quarries.
And then, it may be . . .
                   There is blood on his spurs.

The vendettas of stone that he tamed, the entrail's
intaglio, the recondite
pith of the block, fall behind in his passing,
with the marbles abandoned to night
in a mercy of ruin.
Behind, lie the bridges seen only in dreams,
the citadels armed with his grandeur,
the gardens and courts of his father in the hostile assault,
and the gods of his boyhood alive in the leaves:
there, the faun smiles again, and the ruinous
torso boils up from below like the jet of a fountain.
Light is unveiled: a face that discloses
itself and talks with him suddenly there, turning all to
    delirium.
And the sound of the gallop is heard in a woefuller
measure: a hammer that rises and falls on primordial
    anger.

Unharmed in the potsherds and rubble, behind him
the whole of his architecture leaps, Cyclopean and white
in a furor of forms—cutting arcs in the azure,

subiendo fustes al frontón del cielo,
bajo el ojo asombrado de las cúpulas.
La geometría del espacio llora
una lluvia de líneas trastornadas.
¡Más aún, más aún, más todavía!
Grito del trueno, voz de la centella
que en la mano le rigen.
                    Y galopa.

Atrás, en turbonada, la pintura.
Sube y desciende, palma, esparto, alambre,
el pincel por los ámbitos sin límites.
Precipitada va la anatomía,
viento en escorzo, ardiente alud en guerra.
Suenan portazos en las nubes, treman
rotos los goznes del quicial del mundo.
¡Oh Dios, oh Dios, oh Dios! No sé si infierno
es para mí tu gloria, si tus ángeles
se despeñan en mí como demonios . . .
Y en rasgado ciclón, atrás, hundiéndose,
cartones, cal, esbozos, andamiajes,
muros feroces, convulsivas ánimas.

No es grande la campiña, no es inmensa
la mar, no es grande, no, la solitaria,
ahuyentadora nieve sin vestigios,
no la desarbolada impune noche
para zafar un último relámpago.
¡El mar, tal vez el mar, pero de piedra!
¡Cumbres del mar, mármol del mar, espumas!
¡oh Dios, oh Dios, oh Dios! Va a abrir la mano,
va a arrancarle de cuajo las pupilas
a la luz, va por fin a revelarte
su última luz, dejándote a Tí ciego.
¡Al mar, al mar! Tal vez allí . . .
                    Y galopa.

driving shafts in the heavenly pediments
under the marveling eye of the cupolas.
Geometry weeps in the spacy extension
and falls in a spray of maniacal pointers.
Further: still further and further!
The thunderstone speaks, the voice of the resin and tinder
that bear power to his hand.
                        And he gallops.

Behind, in the hurricane, all that he painted
ascends and descends: the quill of the palm and the flax
and the filament circling the brush in its limitless sweep.
In the thrust of that airy foreshortening, landslides
of luminous anger, anatomy hurtles ahead.
Doors slam in the clouds. The hinges that grappled
the doorposts and joists of the world tremble open.
Merciful God! Shall I say
that your hell is my glory, that your angels
run riot and possess me like demons . . .
A cyclone is parted behind you in splinters and tatters:
plaster and charcoal, scaffolds and chalks and cartoons,
convulsions of spirit, and the barbarous boss on the walls.

The terrain is not infinite, nor the ocean's
immensity. The scarecrow of ice that dissolves
in the wastes of the sea without trace of its passing,
is bounded. The shipwreck of night wears an ultimate
flash in its spars, an impenitent jewel.
Toward the sea, it may be—toward a mineral sea!
Toward the uplands of ocean, the spray and the oceans
    of marble!
Merciful God! He will presently open that hand,
he will pluck out and hold to the light, for Your praise,
the marrow and pith of his eyes. He will discover to You,
    in the end,
the daze of his ultimate levins to blind You forever.
Toward the sea then! Perhaps toward the sea . . .
                        And he gallops.

A Vanished Grove: 6

There, all was like a dream of the past: birds circling the trees long vanished or cut down, burning to sing on the nullified branches; winds searching and shifting eternally in the broom and the furze, alive to a sonorous touch of the air, in the topmost green of the branches; the mouths, the hands, and the foreheads seeking some shadowy well of refreshment, a lover's repose. In that place, all gave back the sound of the past, of the seeding and fall of old forests. Even the light fell like a memory of light, and our infantile games, the truancies of the schoolboy, sounded lost in the depths of the grove.

So, pressing ever more deeply, diminishing myself by degrees, dwindling down to the height of a child, moving further and further away on the journey that brings us at last to that "shadowy gulf" that waits to close over me, I hear in each footfall the advance, the inflexible march of the vanishing groves of my life, like a noiseless invasion.

And, hearing with my eyes and seeing with my ears, I turn with my heart in my mouth, never breaking the obedient march. And the journey fares forward, presses on, night and day, on its stations, overtaking my footsteps, drinking drop after drop of my slumber, drawing into its being the whole of the perishing light, the last darkness of outcries and words.

RETORNOS DE LO VIVO LEJANO
RETURNS OF THE FAR AND THE LIVING

(1952)

Retornos del ángel de sombra

A veces, amor mío, soy tu ángel de sombra.
Me levanto de no sé qué guaridas,
fulmíneo, entre los dientes
una espada de filos amargos, una triste
espada que tú bien, mi pobre amor, conoces.
Son los días oscuros de la furia, las horas
del despiadado despertar, queriéndote
en medio de las lágrimas subidas
del más injusto y dulce desconsuelo.
Yo sé, mi amor, de dónde esas tinieblas
vienen a mí, ciñéndote, apretándome
hasta hacerlas caer sobre tus hombros
y doblarlos, deshechos como un río.
¿Qué quieres tú, si a veces, amor mío, así soy,
cuando en las imborrables piedras pasadas, ciego,
me destrozo y batallo por romperlas,
por verte libre y sola en la luz mía?
Vencido siempre, aniquilado siempre,
vuelvo a la calma, amor, a la serena
felicidad, hasta ese oscuro instante
en que de nuevo bajo a mis guaridas
para erguirme otra vez tú ángel de sombra.

Retornos del amor en los vividos paisajes

Creemos, amor mío, que aquellos paisajes
se quedaron dormidos o muertos con nosotros
en la edad, en el día en que los habitamos;

Returns: Dark Angel

Sometimes I must come as your angel of darkness.
It may happen, beloved, that I wake like an ignorant
beast in a lair, grown sullen and grinding my teeth
on a sword's bitter edges—that blade
whose despairs you interpret so well, my poor darling.
Those are days of my agony, the black hours
of my pitiless coming awake, when I turn
back toward love in the tears
of a spoiled and illicit despondency.
Where the shadows cloud over my life, I know well:
how they close like a noose and draw the knot tighter,
my darling—how they cover your shoulders with darkness,
double them under with darkness, and tear at your life
like a river. No help for it now: I am so for an interval,
when the indelible rock of the past has blinded all vision
and I mangle my force and strive with the rock to destroy
    it,
to win your old freedoms, my darling, and bear you alone
    to the light.
Consumed and defeated, consumed and defeated,
I return to a vagrant repose, a delight
beyond change and vexation—till the moment grows
    darker
again, and I descend to the lairs and the rocks
while the hairs of my head stand on end, like an angel of
    darkness.

Love's Returns: An Inhabited Landscape

Knowing well that the landscapes still slumber,
that the times and the days that we dwelt in, beloved,
fall behind, with our perishing lives;

que los árboles pierden la memoria
y las noches se van, dando al olvido
lo que las hizo hermosas y tal vez inmortales.

Pero basta el más leve palpitar de una hoja,
una estrella borrada que respira de pronto
para vernos los mismos alegres que llenamos
los lugares que juntos nos tuvieron.
Y así despiertas hoy, mi amor, a mi costado,
entre los groselleros y las fresas ocultas
al amparo del firme corazón de los bosques.

Allí está la caricia mojada de rocío,
las briznas delicadas que refrescan tu lecho,
los silfos encantados de ornar tu cabellera
y las altas ardillas misteriosas que llueven
sobre tu sueño el verde menudo de las ramas.

Sé feliz, hoja, siempre: nunca tengas otoño,
hoja que me has traído
con tu temblor pequeño
el aroma de tanta ciega edad luminosa.
Y tú, mínima estrella perdida que me abres
las íntimas ventanas de mis noches más jóvenes,
nunca cierres tu lumbre
sobre tantas alcobas que al alba nos durmieron
y aquella biblioteca con la luna
y los libros aquellos dulcemente caídos
y los montes afuera desvelados cantándonos.

that the trees are oblivious now
and that night has forgotten the splendor that worked
toward the beautiful and promised eternity—

It needs only a leaf's agitation, the breath
of a star we had missed, which returns
with its swift inhalation to restore to our gaze
a bliss brimming over in the coverts that bound us
    together.
Today you awake at my side,
my beloved, in the currants and strawberries of a hidden
recess in the heart of a forest.

There, in the dewy solicitude,
the delicate stir that refreshes your pillow
move the nymphs whose delight turned the wreath for
    your hair,
the mysterious squirrel that climbs on the steeps of the air
and rains down on your sleep all the scrupulous green of
    the branches.

O leaf, be enchanted forever: leaf
whose least perturbation
bears the living aroma
of the blind and the luminous past: let your autumn be
    never!
And you, lost and remotest of stars that now open
an intimate window on my youngest remembrance of
    night—
never fail in your radiance!
Shine still on the bedrooms that dreamed of our childhood
    till dawn.
Shine with the moon on the library,
the delectable book fallen limp on the floor,
the faraway peak standing naked and singing for us, as
    before.

Retornos de una sombra maldita

¿Será difícil, madre, volver a ti? Feroces
somos tus hijos. Sabes
que no te merecemos quizás, que hoy una sombra
maldita nos desune, nos separa
de tu agobiado corazón, cayendo
atroz, dura, mortal, sobre sus telas,
como un oscuro hachazo.
No, no tenemos manos, ¿verdad?, no las tenemos,
que no lo son, ay, ay, porque son garras,
zarpas siempre dispuestas
a romper esas fuentes que coagulan
para ti sola en llanto.
No son dientes tampoco, que son puntas,
fieras crestas limadas incapaces
de comprender tus labios y mejillas.
Han pasado desgracias,
han sucedido, madre, verdaderas
noches sin ojos, albas que no abrían
sino para cerrarse en ciega muerte.
Cosas que no acontecen,
que alguien pensó más lejos,
más allá de las lívidas fronteras del espanto,
madre, han acontecido.
Y todavía por si acaso hubieras,
por si tal vez hubieras soñado en un momento
que en el olvido puede calmar el mar sus olas,
un incesante acoso,
un ceñido rodeo
te aprietan hasta hacerte
subir vertida y sin final en sangre.
Júntanos, madre. Acerca

Returns: A Shadow Accursed

Will it be hard to come back to you, Mother? * Your
seed is grown barbarous. You know
our unworthiness: the damnable
dark that makes strangers of all—dividing
your child from the bosom that grieves for it now,
falling on fiber and marrow, an ax
in the night, atrocious and deadly and obdurate.
Even our hands have disowned us, no longer
our ministers. See how they turn into talons
and claws, hover and slash
at the seals of those fountains
that only your grief could constrain.
The teeth of our heads are as spurs of a precipice,
wild pinnacles pointing
away from your lips and your cheeks.
We are hard-pressed; disaster,
black nights of the soul, denying us vision,
while dawn follows dawn and brings only
a blinded extinction;
untellable horror, things
thought remote from the actual world
on the livid frontiers of our fear:
mother, they happen, they happen.
If you hoped for an aftermath, or
imagined a moment
when the sea might subside or the waves grow oblivious—
the unsleeping vendetta resumes,
the whirling encirclement
that forces us back to the vortex
and vomits us endlessly up to the surface, in blood.
Be with us, Mother. Come close

   * The reference here is to Spain as "mother country" of the poet in exile.

esa preciosa rama
tuya, tan escondida, que anhelamos
asir, estrechar todos, encendiéndonos
en ella como un único
fruto de sabor dulce, igual. Que en ese día,
desnudos de esa amarga corteza, liberados
de ese hueso de hiel que nos consume,
alegres, rebosemos
tu ya tranquilo corazón sin sombra.

Retornos de un poeta asesinado

    Has vuelto a mí más viejo y triste en la dormida
luz de un sueño tranquilo de marzo, polvorientas
de un gris inesperado las sienes, y aquel bronce
de olivo que tu mágica juventud sostenía,
surcado por el signo de los años, lo mismo
que si la vida aquella que en vida no tuviste
la hubieras paso a paso ya vivido en la muerte.

    Yo no sé qué has querido decirme en esta noche
con tu desprevenida visita, el fino traje
de alpaca luminosa, como recién cortado,
la corbata amarilla y el sufrido cabello
al aire, igual que entonces
por aquellos jardines de estudiantiles chopos
y calientes adelfas.

with your flowering bough, now so
precious and secretive, we would seize
with the whole of our yearning; yield yourself back to us
    now,
turn all into blossom and fruit
of sweet savor, equal and single for all. Speed the day
when, all bitterness past, pared
of the rind and the stone, of the gall that infests and
    devours,
we may enter again
your heart's quiet, summer-hearted and cloudless.

Returns: A Poet Murdered
(*F. García Lorca*)

You are here with me now, in the somnolent light
of a deep sleep in March, grown older and mournfuller,
the chalk of your temples and the magical
olive and bronze of your manhood now parched
an unthinkable gray, scored with the passing of years
as if all that was spared to your living identity
was lived to the full in your dying and moved step after
    step in the grave.

Whatever your errand, you were there
in the night, in the glaze
of expensive alpaca, as though recently turned by the
    shears,
with your yellow cravat and amenable
hair to the wind, in the warm oleanders
and a garden's collegiate poplars,
an improvident caller, as always.

Tal vez hayas pensado—quiero explicarme ahora
ya en las claras afueras del sueño—que debías
llegar primero a mí desde esas subterráneas
raíces o escondidos manantiales en donde
desesperadamente penan tus huesos.

                                Dime,
confiésame, confiésame
si en el abrazo mudo que me has dado, en el tierno
ademán de ofrecerme una silla, en la simple
manera de sentarte junto a mí, de mirarme,
sonreir y en silencio, sin ninguna palabra,
dime si no has querido significar con eso
que, a pesar de las mínimas batallas que reñimos,
sigues unido a mí más que nunca en la muerte
por las veces que acaso
no lo estuvimos—¡ay, perdóname!— en la vida.

Si no es así, retorna nuevamente en el sueño
de otra noche a decírmelo.

Retornos del amor en el palco de teatro

Fuera, en la sala, música y luces,
fingido amor, amor que se da en yelo,
en letra muerta, aunque aparentemente
cante sangrando el corazón la vida.

Apagado, llegaba entre cortinas,
oros falsos y rojos terciopelos, el grito
del héroe agonizante a la secreta sombra
del antepalco en donde

Was it your thought—I speak of it
wakefully now—to show me the way
from the underground roots and the fountainheads
under the roots, where your bones
live in anguish—the first of the dead?

                O confess it!
Confess it!
The speechless embrace we exchanged, the tender
address of gesturing me to a chair and seating yourself
at my side with an innocent air, watching
and smiling by turns without speaking a word—
were they not all a trust to reveal your unspoken intent:
See how our niggling encounters and the cant of the past
come to nothing! Death brings us closer together—
tightens the mesh and unites us
—forgive me!—as it never could do in the flesh!

Should dreaming delude me, come back to the night
of my dream and dream me your meaning again.

Love's Returns: A Theater Loge

Beyond, in the orchestra's music and lights,
love is dissembled: love works in the wormwood
and dearth of the word, however
the heart feigns its life or lets blood in an aria.

Past the curtain's red plush and the burst
of the counterfeit gold—a little diminished
at first, the agonist's death rattle climbs a darkened
recess of the balcony,

el amor verdadero, sin palabras,
sin preparados gestos, sucedía.

Eran dulces las manos y los ojos
adivinados, la tibieza umbrosa
de la piel, las rizadas
oscuridades y el silencio lánguido
en la amorosa escena
que los dos, sin aplausos, ofrecíamos
tan sólo al goce de un espejo mudo.

¡Ah, gracia de los años, maravilla
de ofrecerle al amor cualquier penumbra,
la de un coche, una esquina solitaria
o la de un palco de teatro mientras
puede, sin verla, hasta pasar la muerte!

where love, without language, knowing only
the dumb-show of touch, drives toward its need, unrehearsed.

I think of that pathos of hands, of the eyes'
divinations and the shadowy bloom
of the skin, crenellations
of darkness, and the play
that we play in the languishing pause
of the silence—two lovers alone in a mirror,
who offer their joys to the glass, without thought of applause.

O time has its graces; we come bearing wonders
to love: a penumbra
to darken a carriage, a doorway retreat,
or the dark of a theater loge where, unknown to the lovers,
it may be, death had its way in a play and passed over.

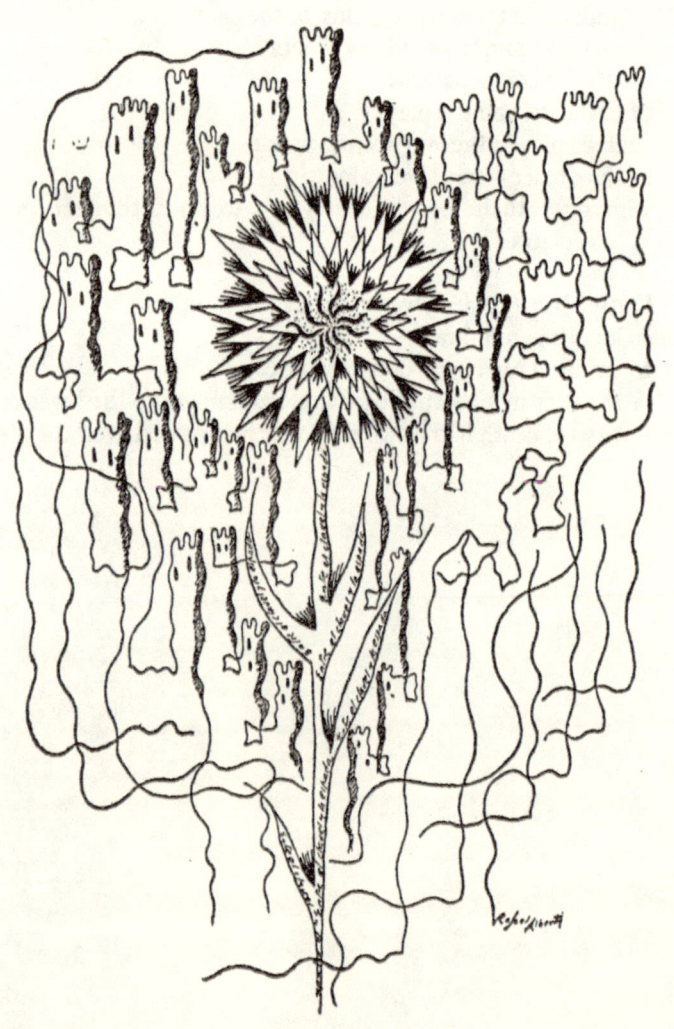

COPLAS DE JUAN PANADERO
BROADSIDES FOR JUAN PANADERO
———————————————————
(1949–1953)

Poética de Juan Panadero

1

Digo con Juan de Mairena:
"Prefiero la rima pobre",
esa que casi no suena.

2

En lo que vengo a cantar,
de diez palabras a veces
sobran más de la mitad.

3

Hago mis economías.
Pero mis pocas palabras,
aunque de todos, son mías.

4

Mas porque soy panadero,
no digo como los tontos:
"que hay que hablar en tonto al pueblo."

5

Canto, si quiero cantar,
sencillamente, y si quiero
lloro sin dificultad.

6

Mi canto, si se propone,
puede hacer del agua clara
un mar de complicaciones.

Juan Panadero: Poetics

1

With Juan de Mairena,*
I say "sparse rhyme is best,"
hardly heard in the verse.

2

In whatever I sing,
ten words are enough
or too many by half.

3

I make my economies.
The little I speak, although terse,
has the sound of my voice.

4

I who put bread on the table, †
am not able to say with the half-wits:
"Talk double-talk to the people."

5

I sing out, if the tune goes that way,
without complications; if I want
to, I weep, let the chips fall where they may.

6

My song, if it pleased me,
would start pure as a waterdrop
and end in a sea of complexity.

* An "apochryphal" creation of Antonio Machado, committed, like Machado, to prosodic austerity and a disavowal of the baroque.
† Juan Panadero, i.e., "Johnny Baker."

7

Yo soy como la saeta,
que antes de haberlo pensado
ya está clavada en la meta.

8

Flechero de la mañana,
hijo del aire, disparo
que siempre da en la diana.

9

Si no hubiera tantos males,
yo de mis coplas haría
torres de pavos reales.

10

Pero a aquél lo están matando,
a éste lo están consumiendo
y a otro lo están enterrando.

11

Por eso es hoy mi cantar
canto de pocas palabras . . .
y algunas están de más.

7

I work like an arrow:
before the poem is poised in the mind,
it has pierced to the circle.

8

Bowman of morning and child
of the air, I draw the string tight
and speed toward a target of light.

9

If the times were less evil,
I would heap up a ballad
like a tower of peacocks, and revel.

10

But matters are otherwise: as I live,
I see this one murdered, that one destroyed,
and another shoveled into a grave.

11

So I keep my line bare
and the melody sparse . . .
and the words make for more.

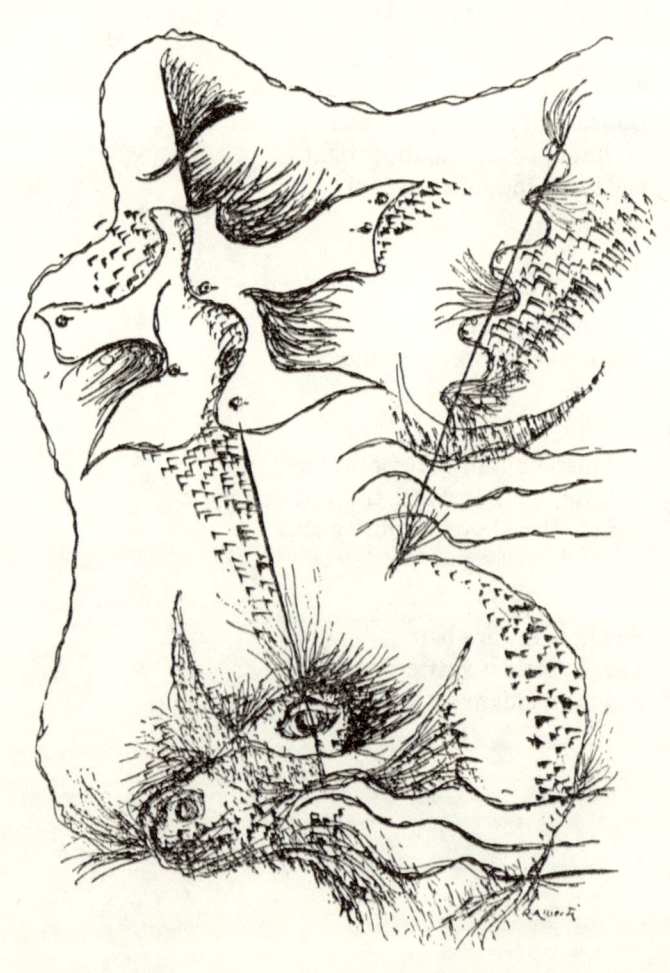

BALADAS Y CANCIONES DEL PARANÁ
BALLADS AND SONGS OF THE PARANÁ

(1953–1954)

The Paraná is one of the three great rivers that form the Plata system in Argentina.

Canción 8

Hoy las nubes me trajeron,
volando, el mapa de España.
¡Qué pequeño sobre el río,
y qué grande sobre el pasto
la sombra que proyectaba!

Se le llenó de caballos
la sombra que proyectaba.
Yo, a caballo, por su sombra
busqué mi pueblo y mi casa.

Entré en el patio que un día
fuera una fuente con agua.
Aunque no estaba la fuente,
la fuente siempre sonaba.
Y el agua que no corría
volvió para darme agua.

Balada del andaluz perdido

Perdido está el andaluz
del otro lado del río.

—Río, tú que lo conoces:
¿quién es y por qué se vino?

Vería los olivares
cerca tal vez de otro río.

—Río, tú que lo conoces:
¿qué hace siempre junto al río?

Song 8

Today the clouds bore me
the winged map of Spain.
How small on the river,
how huge on the meadow and plain
was the shadow it cast!

The shape of the shadow
swarmed with horses; I saw, as it passed,
myself upon horseback, under a shadow,
seeking kinsmen and country again.

I entered the courtyard where once
was a fountain of water.
Nothing remained; but the sound of the fountain's burst
falling, as always, was plain.
And waters long sealed at their source
flowed back, as before, for my thirst.

Ballad of the Lost Andalusian

The lost Andalusian
on the other side of the river.

—River that knows him, say
who he is, what has brought him this way?

He would watch how the olive grows,
it may be, by the banks of a different river.

—River that knows him, say
what he does by the river, day after day?

Vería el odio, la guerra,
cerca tal vez de otro río.

—Río, tú que lo conoces:
¿qué hace solo junto al río?

Veo su rancho de adobe
del otro lado del río.

No veo los olivares
del otro lado del río.

Sólo caballos, caballos,
caballos, solos, perdidos.

¡Soledad de un andaluz
del otro lado del río!

¿Qué hará solo ese andaluz
del otro lado del río?

Search for a war, it may be; discover
the hatred he knew by the banks of a different river.

—River that knows him, say, is it known
what he does by the banks of the river, alone?

—I see only his hut of adobe, looking over
on the opposite side of the river.

But never
the olive groves there on the opposite side of the river.

There are horses and horses, only riderless horses
that strayed from their courses.

And one Andalusian, one
on the opposite side of the river, alone!

One Andalusian. What will he do there, what is left to be
    done
on the opposite side of the river, alone?

www.ingramcontent.com/pod-product-compliance
Lightning Source LLC
Chambersburg PA
CBHW021705230426
43668CB00008B/734